Growing U

MW00986518

By William E. Tudor

Memories of growing up in the 1950's in a small
Indiana town

for Kylie & Shana

and for my friends from the class of 1961 whose pictures
are shown inside and who each died prematurely: Bob
Purkhizer, Ted Bailey, Mike Flowers and Norma Rice

Growing Up in Bluffton

By William E. Tudor

Memoir : *from the French: mémoire from the Latin memoria, meaning "memory", or a reminiscence. Will Rogers put it a little more pithily: "Memoirs means when you put down the good things you ought to have done and leave out the bad ones you did do - from Wikipedia*

Preface

As I grow in years I often find myself wishing that I had spent more time with my parents and grandparents asking them about details of their lives: what they did when they were young, why they did it, what they felt, how they managed life's hardships, etc. The business of genealogy is great, but facts and dates of births, marriages and deaths are a poor substitute for really knowing how things were. In this spirit, I decided to do my part to help my descendants in learning about my upbringing, what I did, and why.

As I began writing I found that my recollections are like my life; an imperfect balance of facts, opinions, truths, half-truths and perhaps a wrongly remembered story that just seemed to fit. Mostly my memoir is about a time and a place, long gone, that is a story of growing up in Middle America after World War II in a small farming community. I hope it reminds you of your beginnings and you find it entertaining.

Bill Tudor,

Roscommon, Michigan

3

Growing Up in Bluffton

Chapter 1

The Beginning

My mother was an independent woman with a long memory for perceived slights. And so, after my brother was born in 1940 in the middle of the coldest January on record and my dad was late to the birth, she hatched her plan. Then, when it was my turn to arrive in November of 1943, she put her plan in action. When her labor pains started she kept quiet till my dad went off to work. Afterwards, when she was sure, she walked down the block to Mary Campbell's white house with the asbestos siding and asked for a ride to the hospital. Mary helped her into the old blue Plymouth like all good neighbors would do and off they went to the hospital for my arrival. When my dad got home from work that day he was surprised to find a note instead of his supper. He soon learned about a new son born earlier that day.

I, of course, learned about this much later. My first recollection about my birth is that I was minding my own business when suddenly someone or something started pushing me around and then, when it seemed things couldn't get any worse, someone started smacking me. I complained bitterly. For some reason, a room full of people thought it funny that I was crying. First, a white coated man smiled, and then several women with white dresses and funny hats started smiling. What with all the smiling going on, I stopped crying and broke out into a smile of my own. That seemed to make things happen and soon thereafter the funny-hat women came to their senses and gave me a blanket and something to eat. I don't remember too much after that.

I spent the normal five days in the hospital after my routine birth while my mother, Anna (Hiester) recovered from the rigors of childbirth. Since she had managed to delay my introduction to my father, Raymond Tudor, he wasn't a central figure in my life for several days. When my mom and I got home from the Clinic Hospital, our family was assisted by my aunt for several days; otherwise my dad would have starved to death since he was pretty much helpless in doing household tasks. [In those days the dads were even more useless than they are today around newborns. It was just as well since my dad claimed to be ignorant of any skill needed for homemaking. This was a common characteristic of men in our town and it no doubt explains my own ineptitude.]

Home was a small house on the south end of Arnold Street in Bluffton, Indiana smack in the middle of Wells County in northeast Indiana. All my important relatives lived in, or near Bluffton, so meeting them was the first order of business. After meeting my dad, I was introduced to my grandparents: Jesse and Cora Hiester, and Ora and Nellie Tudor. Both sets of grandparents were Bluffton residents, the best place in the world to be born, as I was told as soon as I arrived home. In fact, I was told so often about the merits of Bluffton and what a grand place it was to live that I sometimes wondered why anyone would willingly live anyplace else.

I wasn't home from the hospital very long before I was told that the Hiester clan came to Bluffton from a tiny village to the south known as Boundary, Indiana. The name came from the fact that 150 years earlier the village was the site of the boundary between Indian lands and the 'settled' land to the south. The location of the boundary line was chosen by a dashing young man

President William H. Harrison

named William Henry Harrison who convinced Indians to give up their homelands in exchange for cash, some vague promises, and lots of whiskey, watered down, of course. Harrison coerced the treaties because he was a feared warrior. He had learned his craft at the feet of one of the best: "Mad" Anthony Wayne, the General that George Washington appointed to subdue the tribes in the Northwest Territory. Harrison was a young man of promise from a wealthy, well-known family when he was named Aide-de-Camp to General Wayne. Harrison ultimately became one of the most prolific treaty-writers in the young nation, obtaining millions of acres of Indian lands for the new United States government. The government, in turn, sold the new lands to speculators and all manner of land agents eager to make windfall profits in re-selling the lands to farmers.

Both the Hiester and Tudor families moved north from the 'settled' lands in the south to the area in northern Indiana that was given up by the Miami tribe of Indians. The place of my new home, Bluffton, a town in Wells County, is an area 25 miles south of Fort Wayne, Indiana. The namesake of the county was William Wells, also an important figure in the loss of Indian lands.

William Wells was a young boy growing up in Kentucky during the early settlement of that area by Daniel Boone, Simon Kenton and other American pioneers. Wells was kidnapped by Indians and as he grew to maturity he adopted Indian ways and became more Indian than white. He was a slender, red-haired youth who had an athletic bent and he became a favorite of the Indians as he bested many of his peers in shooting arrows, running, jumping, and other feats that Indians considered essential for young braves. Consequently, he had little trouble in convincing a Chief of the Miami tribe that he was a suitable husband for the Chief's daughter. The squaw was Sweet Breeze and the Chief was Little Turtle, leader of a band of Miami. The Miami claimed a large share of Indiana as their homeland including the largest, most important Indian town in the Northwest Territory, Kekionga, later to be known as Ft. Wayne in honor of 'Mad' Anthony Wayne. Little Turtle was the most important Indian in the Northwest Territory and chief adversary of General Wayne. Williams Wells, as Little Turtle's son-in-law and confidant was an important figure among the Indians as they struggled against the whites who wanted their rich lands for farming.

Wells' Kentucky family learned of his whereabouts during the Indian war and arranged a meeting with him in Terre Haute, Indiana. After a series of adventures and with Little Turtle's acceptance, Wells decided to return to white civilization where he subsequently met with General Wayne. Wayne was impressed with the athletic white man who knew more about Middle American Indians than any other white man alive.

A line drawing of the principal figures at the treaty of Greenville where Indians gave up large land allotments in exchange for peace and cash payments

1. Anthony Wayne
2. Little Turtle
3. William Wells
4. William Henry Harrison

Wayne hired Wells to serve as his chief of scouts to help lead the army as they made ready to attack Wells' former Indian tribesmen. Ultimately, Wells was killed by Indians as he rode to rescue soldiers from Fort Dearborn, present site of the city of Chicago. The Indians shot Wells at point blank range and then cut out his beating heart and ate it – it was in Indian tribute to his bravery. A monument to Wells depicting his death is displayed in Chicago.

William Wells owned property and he established a sizable orchard to the north of the old Fort Wayne that the soldiers built. During his life he traveled widely on horseback and in canoes. No doubt he traveled past the future site of Bluffton since the Wabash River was a major means of travel for Indians. When the state of Indiana became organized, the legislators decided to honor Wells and his bravery by naming a county after him. Appropriately, the area along the Wabash River was chosen to honor his memory.

Wells County was quickly settled by pioneering families after the Indians were sent packing by the treaties that Harrison arranged. The soil in and around Wells County with its high clay content held water firmly in place providing crops of all sorts a good place to take root. The relatively mild climate and adequate growing season set the stage for bountiful harvests. It was just what the farmers wanted and so they quickly settled the area all around the Wabash River and a small town they called Bluffton grew there.

The Hiester's migrated to Wells County and settled in Bluffton and Grandfather Jesse Hiester found work in retail, spending most of his life working behind the counter at one store or another. Grandpa Ora Tudor came to Bluffton as a young man and listed his occupation as farmer. He found work initially in a blacksmith shop and helped farmers in shoeing and caring for their horses just after the turn of the 19th century. The town prospered over the years with several manufacturing firms. The most successful at the end of World War II about the time I came along was Franklin Electric, a manufacturer who pumped their way to success with the introduction of just what the U.S. Navy needed, electric motors that would function underwater. Franklin became the town's largest manufacturer and employer about the time I came home from the hospital.

Franklin's success helped to continue the prosperity of the small, northern Indiana town. The county's major activity since the land had been wrested from the Indians 130 years earlier continued to be farming, but the town that grew from it had always been augmented by manufacturing in addition to the marketing and processing of farm produce. The post war boom after 1945 further stimulated business and the town expanded in response. Little Turtle and William Wells wouldn't have recognized the prosperous, growing community that perched on the Wabash River and was tagged as a 'Bluff-town'. My family continued the focus of their forebears: working hard to produce something from the land or the businesses that had settled on it, and so they precisely fit with the area's culture. They welcomed me home from the hospital with confidence that the town and the farming area all around it would be the best place possible for the growing up of a youngster like me.

Chapter 2

Home

Getting home from the hospital meant getting accustomed to my new surroundings. I don't remember much from the first several days since one bed seemed pretty much the same as any other. It wasn't until some months later that things began to take shape around the house as I started looking at the strange things. I kept hearing words but most didn't mean much to me except the terms *milk* and *breast.* They made the most sense when I heard them in the reverse order.

After some months at home I began crawling and understanding something of the word *furniture.* It seemed to me that it was some object that was always in the way of my forward progress. My recall is that furniture and crying seemed to go together.

After a good deal of effort, I learned the layout of our house. It was quite modest by today's standards: a two bedroom, one bathroom, kitchen and front room affair on a standard 50 foot lot. The single bathroom was peculiar in that it had three separate entry doors; the main entry from the kitchen, and then a door to each bedroom. To reach their bedroom, my mom and dad had to first enter the bathroom.

The front room of the house was divided into a dining room and a tiny parlor with its large window overlooking the small front lawn and sidewalk. The dining room portion of the room featured a pot-bellied stove in the corner with its ising glass window and fancy chromed metal work around its big, black, barrel-shaped belly. The free-standing Philco radio occupied its important place nearby with just enough room for the entire family to gather around. The trusty Philco was tuned to our favorite show, *Fibber McGee and Molly* every Wednesday after *The Thin Man*.

I had been home a little more than a year when my dad made a momentous decision. In 1945 the war was going well for the United States and our Allies as U. S. General George Patton rushed toward the homeland, crushing German resistance everywhere. Things were not so rosy in the South Pacific, however, and the U.S. high command anticipated the need for one million troops to invade Japan. Although he qualified for a deferment, Dad decided to do his part and volunteer for the army. He signed the papers and traveled to nearby Ft. Wayne, In. for mustering in with other young men from the county. As the group proceeded through the lines, a ranking officer suddenly ended the process by announcing that the war was over and the new recruits could go home; thus ended Dad's brief entry into the army.

When I was three years old my Grandma Cora Hiester passed away. She was an old lady of 70 and the newspaper announced her death in a one column story printed on the day she died. Death was attributed to heart failure. Mom carefully cut out the newspaper clipping and annotated the date, March 19, 1947, and then put away the clipping for the future. The clipping is yellowed with age but it survives along with all the other clippings Mom saved and it is now in my hands along with another newspaper clipping that I saved: the announcement of my mother's death.

My mother was the baby of her family so my Grandma Cora was much older than my Grandma Nellie. Grandma Cora's death was all very confusing to me at the time; I only understood that my mother and my grandpa were very sad. The event faded quickly in my memory and soon after I started school and a whole new world opened up before me.

I proudly attended Mrs. Speagher's afternoon kindergarten class in September, two months before my fifth birthday. School was held in the brick school building just 3 blocks from home. The walk was even shorter when my big brother Jimmie and I cut through the park that was just one block from home. Our first sight on leaving the tree-lined path from the park was the school and the giant 4th grade boys who controlled the crossing walks. Each boy proudly wore his white safety belt that formed a Z across his chest and waist and he let us know that he was boss of the crossing.

I never knew what the crossing guards were for since we rarely had any cars in the quiet neighborhood. No one drove children to school and many moms like mine didn't drive anyway, so there was virtually no traffic. I always thought the bigger boys were there just to frighten little

Me about 1st grade

kids, that is, until I got to the 4th grade and became a crossing guard myself. I then learned just how important a crossing guard was and how scaring the little kids was a fun thing to do.

The biggest and best thing about attending elementary school was the annual PTA Carnival. For one evening, the entire four classrooms in the school were magically transformed into a, well, a carnival. Each classroom had games you could play and win prizes - really neat stuff like small toys and tiny little games you could stuff in your pocket. And, best of all, was the fishing pond. They had this big curtain and you'd stick your cane pole over the curtain with a pretend hook on the line and, what's that? a tug on the line could only mean something great was on the hook!

After spending all the tickets that Mom gave me to play the games, we retired to the basement where kindergarten was normally held only to find a big table loaded with buns and Sloppy Joes and potato chips and other good stuff. "What? We're going to eat here and not at home? But we always eat at home." I was amazed. The Sloppy Joes were the best ever and my first experience in not eating in the kitchen at home. I felt big, eating at a fancy place with crepe paper laid across the table and all the adults Oooohhing and Aaaahhing over the exhibits their youngsters proudly showed them.

By the end of the first grade and Mrs. Paxson's class, I couldn't wait for summer vacation. I remember only warm, sunny days after school was out for the year. It was great being outdoors and getting rid of those shoes and socks for the summer, making toe jam and going shirtless most days. With no school, I spent most of my time with the other kids in the neighborhood. Mostly, my brother and I would leave home in the morning, find the gang, and then play our favorite games all day long. One of our favorite games was Capture the Flag but we played lots of other games as well that required running through the neighbor's yards, down the street and around the block. All our games were outdoors. If you went indoors for some reason, grown-ups would always ask, "What's wrong, are you sick?"

We had the good fortune to have a full complement of gang members right on our block. There were the Edington's- four brothers, the Noonan's - two brothers, the Shady's, also two brothers and my friend, Billy Campbell, always called by his first and middle name, Billy Dean. Billy Dean lived just down Liberty Street with his grandma, Mary Campbell. All but two of the Edington's were older than me and only Billy Dean was exactly my age. With so many of us available, we could field most sporting teams and we played countless games in all the yards or at the nearby park. Lots of times we made up our own games using cast-offs that we found to play with. Once we made a high jump bar using old bamboo poles that we found in someone's back yard. We stood two poles upright with 20 or 30 nails pounded in each pole and then put another bamboo pole as the cross bar supported by the nails. We had endless contests to see who could jump the highest and land without too much pain in the adjacent sand box.

Most times, our parents never knew exactly where we were. The main rule was that by dinnertime we had to be close enough to hear a shouted call to come home for dinner (except we called it supper). Even though we had the same first names, Billy Dean and I never mistook our calls to come home since Mary had a unique call for him. She had a loud voice, some would say she bellowed like a bull, "Awww Beall" to summon him for his supper. There was no mistaking her call.

The Shady boys had to suffer the indignity of having their mother, a petite woman much given to the finer things, summon them with a bell. It was a crystal glass bell at that. Oh, the shame of it. I knew they hated it but there was nothing they could do. The rest of us, the Edingtons, the Noonans, my brother and me, looked at each other in sadness when the Shadys were called home. I remember thinking that I was happy it wasn't me.

One day, out of nowhere, the Shady boys announced they had learned that the sex act was the reason babies were born. There was dead silence for a moment as we rode our bikes toward town. We all knew about the sex act. We had heard about it countless times in the dirty stories that reverberated around the neighborhood like ping pong balls during a Chinese tournament. At first, none of us believed the Shady boys but they seemed awfully certain of their new information. I remained silent. As one of the younger gang members, I was one of the unbelievers about their story of sex and babies. I held fast in my theory about the stork until my marriage many years later.

In the late 1940's, running with a gang of kids was pretty much accepted behavior, especially when some of the gang members, like me, still wore short pants. [Wearing long pants was a sign of maturity. Little kids always had to wear short pants, probably because they were easier for their mothers to wash.] My dad said he had a gang when he was a youngster in the same south end neighborhood as ours. He had lived only one block away as a boy and had, in fact, lived in only two houses his entire life, less than two blocks apart. His gang was "The South End Dirty Necks." It seemed like a good name to me, but when I suggested

18

it no one liked it, probably because I was the youngest member of the gang.

By the time I reached Mrs. Ritchie's 3rd grade class, most of the boys in the neighborhood, including me, had acquired bicycles. Now we were big shots! In the summertime, the bikes were our means to attend the 'ol swimming hole. It was a former stone quarry, about 2 miles distant, that the Psi Oata Psi society (or some such name) had transformed into a swimming hole. It looked like an abandoned quarry except it had a little sand beach, a concession stand, and two or three lifeguards from the High School. We called it the Si Oats and everyone knew exactly what we meant.

For some reason, Mom and Dad bought Jim and me season tickets to the Si Oats. Almost magically, most of the rest of the gang also got season tickets as well. The result was that every summer afternoon we rode our bikes to the pool for an afternoon of fun. The pool was about two miles from home but the trip seemed a short one as we rode there on summer afternoons, one hour after lunch so's we wouldn't get cramps and drown. 'Course we couldn't swim, so we were forced to watch the bigger kids swim to the raft and lord it over us.

After several weeks of this indignation, I learned how to swim underwater for a few strokes where breathing wasn't necessary. Next came dog paddling - the process of barely keeping your head above water and managing to travel five or six feet before you stood up, exhausted and sputtering out the mouthful of water that came in when you opened your mouth to breathe too soon. As I got better I began to wonder if I could end the indignity of being confined to the shallow end of the pool with the little kids by dog-paddling to the raft. On one fateful day in late summer I decided to try. I took a deep breath and passed under the chain separating the kiddy area from the deeper part. Off I went as my feet suddenly passed the area where I could still touch bottom. I dog-paddled as hard as I could but my face kept slipping under the water, sometimes when I needed to breathe.

I made it only a quarter of the way to the raft before I realized I didn't have enough air to make it all the way, what with the amount of water I was taking in. I turned around and headed back toward the chain. Taking a large gulp of air I pushed myself underwater and began swimming for all I was worth. I surfaced when my hand hit the chain. Safe!, my feet brushed the bottom. "I think I'll wait a little longer before I try that again," I said to myself.

Chapter 3

Big Ears & Big Changes

Sometime in 1949 I awoke from a sound sleep and went to the bathroom that was just a few steps from my little bedroom. Shortly after I got back in bed I could hear the sounds of someone else in the bathroom. It was my father. The reason I could hear him is because he was talking to my mother in their bedroom only a few feet distant. I remember his words distinctly: "Are you sure you want to have another baby?" he asked. I don't remember anything else and I went back to sleep. I don't know why that particular memory stayed with me. I only know that some months later, in 1950, a new baby girl was born into our house. My father named her Linda Kaye Tudor. She was to be so known, he insisted, not as Linda, but as Linda Kaye. After I heard that, I was relieved that I wasn't known as Billy Bob or some such fool thing.

Some months after the pregnancy was obvious, Dad had another surprise for us. At supper one evening, as the four of us were sitting at the kitchen table, he announced that we were going to have, not a cellar, but rather, a proper basement in our house. He practically chortled as he told about the plan and my mother nodded agreeably. "And, the best part is, the new basement means we will have hot water right from the tap! No more heating water on the stove for us!" he beamed. Now I didn't know everything as a 3rd grader, but I KNEW that basements didn't cause hot water. I figured the old man was losing it what with the new baby and all. I decided to remain silent since that was the best policy most of the time with the old man as he didn't have a lot of patience with a little kid like me.

Early that spring work on the new basement began. He dug and the rest of us helped carry out buckets of dirt. He was excavating under our house, just inside the foundation. It was slow work as the soil was a hard, grey clay that required a pickaxe to loosen. His plan was to excavate under the entire house to an eight foot depth to provide a basement with room for new plumbing, a new furnace and other essentials for a modern home. As the work progressed he finally realized the pickaxe wasn't doing the job so he arranged to borrow an air hammer and air compressor to help in breaking up the hard clay. The air hammer made if faster, not easier. It must have been around this time that he decided that an eight foot ceiling was not a necessity for a small basement that was rapidly becoming a cellar.

Finally, the basement was finished and he was correct, it did mean hot water right from the tap as a plumber installed a hot water heater and drains so Mom could do the washing in the basement. No more heating water on the stove at bath time! Unfortunately, this innovation in our household led to a decided disadvantage for me as the once-a-week Saturday baths were replaced by more frequent bathing. Next, the furnace man came. We said goodbye to the old pot-bellied stove in the front room and hello to a brand new coal-fired furnace. The coal furnace needed coal, of course, so that meant a coal bin in the basement also. The coal bin was a small room built of two by four lumber positioned just under the little basement window that had been cut into the foundation. That fall, the coal delivery truck came to our house for the first time and I watched the black-faced men as they drove their truck right up into our yard, opened the little window and began shoveling coal into the bin. Coal dust rose into the air as they shoveled and I learned first-hand why their eyes looked so white against their black faces. It was a surprise when they took off their gloves to reveal white skin. Every part of their skin and clothes were black from the coal dust. They had the dirtiest job in town.

Mom was generally in charge of keeping the furnace in operation while the rest of us were in school or at work. She would go to the basement several times a day and shovel coal into the furnace to keep the fire going. If the fire went out, it was a big job to restart it and a chill would settle over the house. Consequently, in fear of letting the fire go out, she would have a roaring fire going most of the time. Sometimes, her fire was going at such a roar that we had to open the back door to cool things off! She didn't like it if anyone complained and so it became a big joke about us wanting to heat the outside.

The new baby girl in the house didn't have much of an impact on me as I was excited about school. The summer before the 4th grade was a heady time for me. Our school, the Park Elementary School, only had 4 grades and it was finally my turn at the top. I had learned all about the social structure at school and it was finally my turn to be the big cheese, the top of the heap, the big boy on the playground, so to speak. Maybe I would even get a girlfriend like some of the other boys I knew who counted six or seven separate girl friends. No doubt I would be assigned to be a school crossing guard where I could boss around the little kids on their way to school.

The only downside to the fourth grade was that I had to master the multiplication tables and I had to submit to the iron-fisted rule of our 4th grade teacher, old Mrs. Bender. By the time I reached 3rd grade, I knew all about old Bender. She was the object of our scorn and even the 3rd grade boys knew the poem that some clever student had made up about her.

'Ol Miss Bender, fat and tender, skinny in December

It never seemed to occur to any of us that the poem about Mrs. Bender should actually make any sense.

Mrs. Bender was a thin, short little wisp of a woman who was assigned the dual role of School Principal and teacher of the 4th grade. She always wore long dresses and flat shoes and she rarely smiled as she towered over the boys and girls with her short, coal-black hair framing her oval face and glasses. Each year from 2nd grade onward, Park School students had been working on numbers and the multiplication tables. It was no secret that Mrs. Bender required all her students to master the times tables or they couldn't be promoted.

I hated the dreaded times tables. I could never seem to get the right answer and it didn't make any sense to me why we needed to memorize and then sing out, " blank times blank is blank" just because 'ol Mrs. Bender asked. She required the times tables all the way through the 12's! It seemed an impossible task as I would forget the answers from one day to the next. When it was time to recite, I always scrunched down in my desk chair, hoping she wouldn't call on me. One day 'ol Bender finally must have caught on to my scrunching down trick 'cause she called on me.

"Alright Billy, what is six times seven? " she asked with a suppressed grin, knowing she probably would be seeing me repeat the 4th grade.

"42," a strange voice answered.

It took me a moment to realize the voice was my own. I had actually given the right answer! I hadn't even thought about the answer and it came out just like that. I sat in silent amazement. 'Ol Bender seemed as surprised as me and she turned away quickly, refusing to show her disappointment that I got the answer right. From that day on the multiply answers just seemed to pop up whenever I needed them. Somehow, I had foiled old Bender!

On sunny summer days after old Bender, when the days were long and the humidity was higher than the clouds floating above, swimming was the main attraction and, as usual, I spent lots of time at the Si Oats. The raft in the deep part of the Si Oats swimming hole, some 40 to 50 yards from shore, was the undeniable attraction for those of us who could swim that far. Floating on 25 feet of water, the wooden raft was covered with carpet and could accommodate a dozen or more swimmers lounging about. When several members of the gang were there, we always started a game we called water tag. In this game, several boys would form a team and dive into the water while one or more would remain on the raft. Those in the water would try to return to the raft without being touched by those on the raft. The rule was that the raft people were required to dive into the water and race underwater toward the swimmer like a torpedo. Anyone touched by the torpedo diver in this fashion was 'It', and then required to take his turn on top the raft.

The way the game worked was that those of us in the water would try and stay beyond the reach of the divers, but we would quickly tire of trying to keep our heads above water while doing the dog paddle and thus be forced to return to the raft, swimming as quickly as possible to avoid the divers. Day after day as we played the game, we improved our swimming skills and our stamina. The divers, for their part, learned to take deep breaths and cruise for long distances underwater. And so it was, as the long, lazy summer days walked toward fall, I improved my swimming skills along with some of the other South End Dirty Necks.

One of the terrible diseases during my growing up was epilepsy. It was common enough that it seemed as though everyone knew someone who was afflicted and it was not too uncommon to see a convulsion (we called it a 'fit') where the victim would fall to the ground and writhe about unconsciously, foaming at the mouth and making strange groaning sounds. The only treatment during convulsions was trying to prevent the patient from hurting himself. Other than placing a handkerchief in the mouth to prevent a sufferer from biting his tongue, most times bystanders just stood around helplessly until the epileptic fit passed after several minutes. Unfortunately, epilepsy seemed to be one of those diseases that people were ashamed of and most of the sufferer's kept their disease hidden until a convulsion in public made it impossible to conceal.

One afternoon I was swimming and the pool was crowded as usual. In the hot summer sun the crowd of swimmers, watched intently by the lifeguards, seemed to be in constant motion from beach to concession stand. As usual, I was on the raft with several 'Tag' regulars as well as a number of other swimmers. Suddenly the lifeguard blew his whistle and the crowd quieted. I stood motionless and looked around. I didn't see anything out of the ordinary but the lifeguard ordered everyone out of the water. The swimmers in the shallow beach area quickly waded out of the water while those of us on the raft waited to see if the lifeguard wanted us to leave the raft or stay put.

I looked toward the shore to see the lifeguard swimming toward the raft as hard as he could go. As he approached the raft I heard someone say, "He went down over there!" I looked to see the speaker pointing at a spot in the water on the far side of the raft. Suddenly, time seemed suspended as the lifeguard climbed onto the raft, out of breath, but gesturing toward those of us on the raft. He knew many of us from our daily visits to the pool and our incessant game on the raft. After the lifeguard asked us to dive down and find the boy, I deduced that someone had fallen off the raft and hadn't surfaced.

The lifeguard and six or seven of us on the raft began diving toward the bottom with our hands extended in hopes of reaching and rescuing the youngster. I dove in and rushed toward the bottom, holding my breath as long as I could. I couldn't see a thing nor did I reach the mucky bottom some 25 feet down.

I surfaced to find other boys gasping for breath just as I was. We climbed back on the raft for another dive into the inky blackness and another failure. By the third time I climbed on the raft, I heard the cry of sirens and almost simultaneously, another diver cried out that he had the boy. I saw the swimmer struggling to hold an arm in the air, while the rest of the torso was still underwater. In a moment, several hands lifted the motionless body onto the raft. In a minute more, firemen in a boat set out from the beach toward the raft. I was dispatched from the raft toward the beach to help in landing the returning boat. As the firemen drew near with the white-faced boy lying unconscious in the boat, I heard one of them say, "He's a goner."

After the sounds of the sirens and excited voices of the divers and lifeguard, it was eerily silent as the motionless boy was carried from the boat and loaded into the waiting ambulance. No one spoke and no one seemed to be in a hurry.

In the several minutes between the times he had fallen into the water and his body was recovered, the young boy had drowned. I learned later that he was an epileptic and that he had a sudden convulsion on the raft and fell into the water. I had been in the water at the time and hadn't seen him fall. His death rocked the community and the newspaper carried a full account of the accident. His house was on my paper route so I had to walk by it each day. Swimming lost much of its luster for the rest of that summer and at night, in bed, I dreamt about diving into the water, over and over, in search of the lost boy. I never found him in my dreams just as I had never found him at the pool.

During those early years in elementary school my playtime was occasionally interrupted by must-do chores. The most time-consuming chore I had to do on occasion was to help my Grandma, Nellie Tudor. Grandma Nellie and Grandpa Ora lived two blocks from my house on a 2 acre patch of ground at the very edge of town. On their two acres they had berry bushes, apple trees, chickens, a pig, a cow, and a large vegetable garden plus Grandma's flowers that ran the length of their driveway. Grandma appreciated any help she could get with the range of tasks that she faced as a homemaker. She also worked as a housecleaner for two or three families and she was active in her church so she was a busy woman.

Grandma Nellie Tudor

At various times, I was enlisted to help with the flowers, the berries, and the chickens. I didn't particularly like helping with the chickens. The chicken coop always stank, the chickens liked to peck at me, and the work was generally disagreeable. One of the worst jobs with the chickens was when Grandma decided it was time to whitewash the coop. [For those who don't know, whitewash was a low-cost, smelly coating made from lime, chalk and water that was applied to interior walls as a substitute for paint.] The procedure for the whitewashing job was to first chase the chickens from the coop (my job) and collect any eggs in their nests (another of my jobs) before the real work of cleaning out the coop. The coop was full of poop. Chicken poop is about the worst smelling stuff you can imagine. Grandma used straw on the nests and so the coop was full of straw that the chickens managed to scatter everywhere and the straw was full of poop. Actually, there was poop everywhere. Grandma did most of the hard work as we swept and shoveled out the mess. After all that it was finally time to apply the whitewash to the walls and the nests. The chickens had to stay outdoors for that day until the whitewash dried.

The saving part of the chicken coop job was that it took so long I always had lunch with Grandma. She made things for lunch that I liked including a pitcher of freshly made lemonade with one or two peels floating in the pitcher along with several ice cubes. After the stuffy air in the coop it was refreshing to sit in the lawn with our lemonade and lunch consisting of bowls of soft boiled eggs with chunks of butter floating on top and a piece of homemade bread. Grandma liked cookies so we often had a cookie or two with lunch also. She liked butter also and sometimes she would put a dab of butter on her cookie.

The other chicken job I helped with on occasion was when Grandma decided to fry a chicken for a Sunday dinner or for some other special occasion. My job was to help with the butchering and plucking. She sometimes asked me to 'corral' a bird and direct it to her. I was generally able to avoid this job because I didn't like to be the one to choose which bird was going to be butchered for our dinner. Ultimately, she would catch the bird by its legs and then hold it against a chopping block that always sat outside the coop. Whop! And it's head was off by the trusty hatchet that she carried. Afterward, she would drop the bird and I forever learned the meaning of the phrase, *"running around like a chicken with its head cut off."* I quickly learned to stand back after she dropped the headless bird. The birds ran about the area in crazy circles, flapping their wings violently for 30 seconds or more. Suddenly, the luckless bird would stop and drop dead – plop! - just like that.

Plucking the chicken was another bad job. After the bird fell dead, we would grab the bird and pull big handfuls of white feathers and toss them in the garbage unless Grandma needed them for a new pillow. Next we tackled the bird's pin feathers, those tiny little feathers next to the bird's skin. Grandma had carried a bucket of boiling hot water to the coop area and she would plunge the bird into the hot water to help in teasing out the tiny pin feathers. After that, she would clean the bird and disjoint it for the frying pan. She floured the pieces and then fried her chicken in lard using a cast iron fry pan with a blazing fire underneath it. The grease would pop and sizzle as the floured meat turned a golden brown. It tasted so good that I was able to forget my revulsion at the process of getting the bird from the coop to the kitchen.

Grandpa took care of the pig and the cow and I didn't have to help other than mucking out the stall once or twice. The cow pasture was nearly one acre in size, about half of the property. It was a rectangular piece and the driveway to the barn ran alongside the pasture. Grandma had a long flower bed next to the driveway, right by the cow pasture. She and the cow had a running battle over her flowers. As the flowers began growing in the spring the cow would bide his time until they blossomed and were tall enough for him to reach over the fence and nibble. Of course he always seemed to nibble on only the nicest ones, at least, that's what Grandma said. She was too religious to swear, but I know she was thinking swear words as she grumbled about that awful cow and his eating habits when he had a perfectly good pasture field.

Grandpa and Grandma kept animals to eat and they never seemed to be concerned about making pets of the animals. My Grandpa always named his cows, sometimes naming them Billy or Jimmie. He would buy a young animal and then keep it for a year or two before fattening it on the combination of his pasture and purchased grain. In the fall, the cow would be butchered for his table and ours. The butchering never seemed to bother Grandpa even though he called the cow by name, fed him by hand and even curried him on occasion. Grandma similarly seemed to have no compunction about cutting the heads off her chickens. I didn't like it that the animals had to be killed to feed us so I tried not to think about it, especially the chickens since we ate a lot of Sunday dinner chickens. I also thought Grandma was a little cruel in the way she killed the birds until my dad told me that it took him the longest time to convince Grandma to use the hatchet: earlier she had simply rung their necks.

Chapter 4

Me and Jimmie

Besides going to school and playing, I spent most of my free time as an elementary school youngster with my older and bigger brother Jim. Even though he was almost four years older, we went almost everyplace together: elementary school, Sunday school, the playground, the neighborhood, the swimming pool, etc. As we grew, he was always exposed to the growing up changes first. When we moved from one elementary classroom to another, he was first. When we went to Daily Vacation Bible School, he was first. When we 'graduated' from tricycles to bikes, he was first. By the time it was my turn to experience those new things he was an old hand at it and he showed me the ropes. I probably heard my first dirty joke from him. So, what did he get from me for leading the way into our big new world and taking me by the hand? - mostly grief.

Jim and I spent a great deal of our time together fighting. Our disagreements and arguments, no matter how small, always led to an out and out battle. We fought almost anytime, anywhere. Surprisingly, we had specific procedures leading up to our fisticuffs. First, an argument would escalate into a shoving match. Next came a punch, always first on the upper arm, with a rather a reduced force. We took turns on the punches, each of us gauging the severity of the blow and responding with a slight increase of force. After three or four blows, one of us would become enraged and lunge toward the other intent on taking him to the ground where the blows could become more effective. By this time the fight was in high gear and was accompanied by shouts and crying which would normally bring an adult to bear on the disagreement and end the battle.

During those early years of my growing up we probably had two or three thousand fights. Mom was most often the referee as Dad was away from home Monday through Friday at his job as a carpenter. I can only recall two of the fights in vivid detail; the first because a neighbor intervened instead of mom or dad.

Jim and I were outdoors in the garage where dad had installed a basketball hoop so we could play basketball inside in bad weather. The smooth concrete floor made a pretty good surface so we played there even in nice weather; mainly because we didn't have an outdoor place to play that was nearby. It was warm on the day of the big fight so we had the big, crème-colored door to the garage wide open. Our neighbor, Ida Moser, was in her backyard placidly smoking her bees before removing the honey combs that she sometimes shared with us. Something happened, I don't remember what, but it was enough to upset one of us who happened to have the prickliest attitude at that moment. A fight ensued that quickly became a wrestling match and once again, Jim seemed to get the upper hand. Ida apparently wasn't used to hearing children screaming bloody murder, so she sat down her smoker and came closer for a look at the commotion. Aghast at what she saw, she ran screaming to Mom that Jim had me pinned to the floor and was banging my head against the concrete. In deference to Ida, Mom came to the garage and made us stop. I thought she broke up the fight prematurely because I wasn't losing by that much and I still had a chance. Neither the floor nor my head was too much the worse for wear and in 15 minutes both Jim and I had forgotten the entire episode.

The other memorable fight occurred between Jim and me on a camping trip. We had made arrangements with the Shady family that Jim and I would accompany the two boys, Ted and Norman, on our first-ever overnight camping trip. The Shady's had an uncle who owned a farm. The farm had a small wood plot, no more than three or four acres, surrounded by cultivated fields on all sides. To us boys growing up in Indiana where the belief was that every acre of land should be cultivated and harvested, his small patch of woods was a forest wilderness that surely contained all manner of wild creatures. We hadn't learned that Hoosier farmers had killed or chased out every large creature that could do them harm 150 years earlier. (When Daniel Boone was roaming about Kentucky he encountered bison, elk, bear, etc. The animals counted all the states making up the Northwest Territory as their homeland. Sadly, by 1850, the last of the big game was extirpated from Indiana as the farmers joyfully cultivated every available spot.)

The camping trip had all the earmarks of a huge success. We had spent days planning our food, assembling our gear and getting ready for the big event. Finally, the big day arrived and we trudged through the cornfields to the woods overloaded with gear. After a short time we found the ideal spot to pitch the tent that would accommodate the four of us. It was a small opening in the oak and maple forest with big trees on all sides; just right for our tent. We laid out the tent canvas, hoisted it on two wooden poles and then staked down the sides by hammering wooden pegs into the soft clay soil. Next, we stowed our bedrolls, each made up of old blankets pinned together in a rectangular shape and then positioned our food supply, just so, adjacent to the tent. Finally it was time for the most important job of all, making the privy. We couldn't find any other small openings in the woods so we decided that the place to dig a hole for use in burying our waste was pretty much right next to our camping site. Jim and I took to the shovels and in short order we had a hole large enough to accommodate the excrement of an entire herd of cows. Ted and Norman chopped off some tree branches with their hand axe to place over the hole and serve as a toilet seat and viola! - Our privy.

The campout was going great. No one had bothered us and we were deep in the woods on our own, free to do whatever we wanted . . . almost. The only limit to our newfound freedom lay within our own society, that is, by the strictures that we put on each other in our attempt to get along. There was the rub. Jim and I experienced a disagreement about some aspect of our camping that led to an argument. Ted and Norman, unaccustomed to our ways, refused to take part in the disagreement and stood apart from us. The argument escalated and soon a fight broke out. This one was a little different because we had no adult to break up the fight and the supplies for our camping trip were no match for our rambunctious behavior. As we charged at each other, one of us knocked over the store of food, spilling the milk. It meant little compared to the terrible injustice that we each felt and the fight continued as a wrestling match. Next to suffer from our argument was the tent. We rolled about the ground, into the stakes, into the tent poles and the tent came crashing down on top of the two of us.

This fight had become a real free-for-all and Ted and Norman stood in silence. Finally the fight ended when we were each equally disadvantaged with a tent laying over us and the prospect of camping without a tent loomed large. Ted and Norman helped put everything back together. The fight was forgotten about as quickly as it began and the camping trip was a great success as we cooked our hot-dogs and slept peacefully next to our wonderful privy. The next morning the Shady's aunt and uncle treated us to breakfast in their farmhouse and we had home-made pancakes with butter melting on top and fresh cold milk.

The other thing that Jim and I did together was to get sick. We passed germs back and forth faster than the south-bound freight train zipping through town. Consequently, we shared colds, head lice, influenza, chicken pox, measles and mumps just to name a few. Mumps may have been the most serious disease and we were constantly told to lie down and rest or "the mumps can go down on you." I didn't know what that meant, but it sounded bad, and so I stayed in bed several days even though it was a hard thing for me to do.

The most dangerous malady that we both encountered was ringworm. As we now know, the fungus that left ring-shaped bumps in our scalps was not particularly dangerous, but the treatment to eradicate the fungus was infinitely more so. We had our heads shaved and we had to wear tight-fitting skull caps during our treatment. The main part of the treatment was X-ray irradiation to kill the fungus, a highly effective method. I remember sitting in a darkened room with a blue-white glowing light being passed over my scalp. The dosage of the X-ray used was about 1,000 times more than is currently allowed. [In one study with children from Israel, 6,000 died after 100,000 children were irradiated. Cancer is one of the consequences of receiving high dosages of X-rays.] After our treatment the ringworm went away and we were never bothered by it again. The source of the ringworm was unknown, but it was suspected that barbers passed it from one person to another before they began using UV radiation for sterilizing their tools.

Home remedies were really big in our family. The home remedies my mother used were so disagreeable it was actually a dangerous thing to be sick around our house. I generally tried to hide my symptoms from my mother so that I would be spared her home remedies that were worse than the sickness. For instance, if you dared complain of a sore throat, quick as a wink she would whip up a concoction that she called a poultice. She would pour some foul-smelling, goopy stuff on a rag (I remember raw egg on one occasion), liberally dose it with pepper or some other herbal remedy, and then wrap it around your neck, pin it in place and demand that you wear it all day long. The remedy was always worked. After wearing the messy, smelly thing all day long, I always said that I was much better.

Her remedies for other ailments were equally disagreeable. Common colds required either a mustard plaster or liberal doses of Vicks Vapor Rub on the chest and neck. This treatment probably helped avoid the spread of cold germs as no one would want to get too close to anyone who smelled like Vicks Vapor Rub all day long. Stomach distress of any kind always called for a laxative or, worse yet, an enema. After suffering through several enemas using her soap and water solution, I never complained about stomach upset and I tried hard never to burp or pass gas if she was listening. No one ever farted in our house as Mom's sensibilities were too refined for such bodily functions. There were lots of examples of gas-passing but all were characterized by other names. The most common name that Mom favored was 'poogie-bar.' Based on my upbringing, I thought the term poogie-bar was rather refined English until I went to college.

If I had an ailment that Mom was uncertain about, she would sometimes revert to asking her father, Jesse Hiester, or my Grandmother Nellie about an appropriate remedy. That was about the worst thing she could do in my judgment. Those old folks had even stranger remedies than my mother. Grandma Nellie always seemed to favor the use of paregoric (camphorated tincture of opium – given to children for diarrhea or in the case of my Grandma, it could be used for just about anything if nothing else seemed to work). The Hiesters also had a strange assortment of home remedies that my mother was forced to take when she was growing up. For some reason they thought it wise to 'thin the blood' in the fall and the appropriate tonic was a tablespoon of coal oil. Apparently it is true, "that which doesn't kill you makes you stronger," since both my parents survived this kind of medicine.

Chapter 5

At Home

Our family life had a rhythm that varied with the season. In the spring the main family focus was putting out the garden, that is, tilling the soil and sowing the seeds. This occupied much of the spring as it often had to be repeated when the seeds were sown too early and a late spring frost occurred. My dad would begin the process by turning over the soil with a shovel. Working in the evenings and on Saturdays, it took him two or three weeks to complete since most of our back yard was a garden. One year, he hired a man to come to our yard with a team of horses to till the soil and I watched from the house as the big draft horses completed the job in a couple hours. After that, dad bought a tiller. I didn't have too much to do with the planting; it was too important a job for a little snot-nosed kid to be involved. Mom and Dad planted all manner of vegetables: onions, potatoes, beans, peas, radishes, beets, tomatoes, etc. In the fall, Mom preserved the vegetables by canning them.

Summertime was the time for playing. We played outdoors from the time we got up and left the house until it was time for the evening meal. When I was in elementary school, I didn't have too many jobs to do in the summer. As the summer waned things changed and I had to help with the vegetables and the raspberries. Even though I was little, I could do jobs like picking peas and shelling them, and snapping green beans. I helped under protest and under the supervision of Mom who had to keep watch less I leave for playing with someone who happened by. One of the jobs that I had was that of delivering raspberries. My mother kept a patch of both red and black raspberries and she sold a few quarts to our neighbors. My job was to deliver the berries.

I spent quite a little time calling on the neighbors for one reason or another. Before we had a phone, children were used to pass messages back and forth around the neighborhood. Gossip wasn't big but news about sickness and other family emergencies was a topic deserving of a messenger. Generally, the recipients of this kind of news would, as often as not, prepare a dish of food to send along to the family with the emergency. Another door-to-door job that fell to me or my brother was collecting money for flowers for funerals. Whenever anyone died (it seemed like a weekly event to me), the job was to canvas the neighborhood and solicit money for flowers for that person's funeral. No one ever refused to contribute so our neighborhood must have been well-known among the flower shops in town.

Playtime was drastically curtailed in the fall when school began. Mom was busy with the gardens and canning vegetables and sometimes I was pressed into service snapping green beans or shelling peas of something similar. I could tell the long summer days were coming to an end as we walked to school each morning and then walked home again for lunch. Walking home after school meant listening to the Cicadas as they buzzed their monotonous tune to announce that fall was here and winter was coming. Although we played outdoors most days during the summer and fall, our wintertime activities were mostly indoors so none of us ever learned to skate on the ice or ski in the snow.

Other things changed in the dead of winter as Dad would be home instead of being gone most of the week. Most winters his company laid off their carpenters since the construction jobs required warmer weather for making cement into concrete. For several winters running, Dad worked on our house adding a back porch, expanding the living room, adding a basement and finally, converting a portion of the attic to an upstairs bedroom. It was exciting to see these changes. Like many of the other houses in our south end neighborhood ours was a modest home. Since the original house was so small, the changes Dad made dramatically affected our lifestyle.

In addition to the seasonal rhythms, our life had a weekly pattern that changed little from week to week and it was directed mainly by the household tasks that Mom managed. Monday was wash day; she gathered all the clothes worn during the week and washed them in her washing machine. After washing she would run the clothes through two rubber rollers called wringers, to wring or squeeze water from them before hanging them outside on the clothesline. The clothes were hung out to dry even in cold weather. If it was cold enough to freeze, she would leave them outside until they froze or nearly froze and then bring them inside and drape them over every available piece of furniture to finish drying. After she got her new basement, Dad put clotheslines across the basement ceiling and she was able to hang the damp clothes there in cold weather until she got a gas-fired clothes dryer some years later.

Tuesday was ironing day. The cotton fabrics used in those days were not treated in any way to reduce wrinkling and they came from the clothesline in a mass of wrinkles. No respectable person would wear wrinkled clothes so ironing was an essential part of doing the laundry. Since the fabrics weren't treated with sizing or 'no-iron' agents, ironing was a lengthy, laborious process. One thing that helped a little in reducing the time spent ironing was the use of stretchers, a stiff wire assembly that could be inserted in pant legs to stretch the fabric and help make the crease in the front of the trousers. Even with stretchers, ironing was much more difficult than with today's fabrics.

Starching clothes during or after the wash also made ironing important. Many of the garments had to be starched to hold their shape and conform to the fashions of the day. [*Starching* was name applied to the process of soaking a garment in a water solution containing starch. Upon drying, the starch would make the garment stiff. Most times it was so stiff that it would scratch and irritate a young boy's neck, making him wish the process had never been invented.] Men's shirt collars on Sunday clothes, for example, were always starched to provide a stiff, upright shape that would fit closely around a man's neck.

Mom used to iron for our family and then also iron for a couple of single men who would pay to have their shirts ironed. She received 15¢ a shirt and it took around 20 minutes per shirt so she earned about 50¢ for an hour's work. If the ironing was finished by Wednesday, Mom would work on other household tasks until Saturday.

Saturday was bath day. By the time I got to elementary school, I washed myself in the tub although my mother washed my back and checked me over to make sure I had washed my hair and behind my ears. After the weekly bath, we were expected to keep clean by washing with a washrag at the sink in the bathroom. It was pretty easy to stay clean in the winter and pretty hard in the summer since I played in the dirt barefooted much of the time and often shirtless as well.

Sunday was church day. Sunday morning I had to put on my best clothes for Sunday school before we walked to church. The church was on Mulberry Street, four blocks distant from our house. We went to the church on Mulberry Street because it was where my Grandma Nellie went and it was the church that my dad had grown up attending. Grandma was a devout Christian who had attended the Mulberry Church for most of her life. It was a small, brick building with a steeple on the front like the kind that you see in pictures. Inside was a single large room with a level floor and a slightly elevated front area where the minister stood behind a pulpit to preach. Also in front were a piano on one side and a small organ on the other side, each behind a low wooden fence varnished in the same amber color as the pews. The room was painted white and it was filled with long oak pews on either side of an aisle down the center of the room. The walls had six tall windows, three on each side.

The church was a Wesleyan Methodist Church, an offshoot of the larger, better known Methodist Church. The Wesleyan Methodist Church had an auspicious beginning; it split from the Methodists at an organizing meeting in New York in 1843 over the question of slavery. The Wesleyans wanted to abolish slavery whereas the Methodists were less inclined to raise a ruckus over the issue. Accordingly, a group of ministers established the new church that expanded, moved west and eventually merged with other denominations to become a world-wide church. Surprisingly, their headquarters were and are in a small town in Indiana, despite the presence of Wesleyan churches around the world.

The Wesleyan Methodists followed many of the Methodist traditions, except that they emphasized the notions of hell-fire and damnation and the need for 'being born-again' to attain a state of holiness required for eternal life. Many of the members of the church were very conservative. The ladies from this group shunned all jewelry and any sort of make-up. One of the girls about my age was required by her conservative parents to wear only long black stockings and plain long dresses. For these folks, most forms of entertainment were unholy and movies were strictly forbidden. They seemed to think that if it was fun, it was probably sinful.

My Grandma was a deeply devout lady and she believed implicitly in all that the church preached. Grandma Nellie attended Sunday morning services and Sunday evening services as well as Wednesday night prayer meeting. Grandpa believed not at all and refused to attend. My dad seemed somewhat ambivalent about the beliefs of the church, but he attended regularly in consequence of Grandma's beliefs and attendance. Perhaps as a compromise, our family attended only Sunday school and never stayed for church service that was held immediately after Sunday school. Sunday school was enough for me as the church service preaching and proselytizing sometimes spilled over into Sunday school.

The church was a scary place when I was little. On occasion, the minister would ask people to testify, an invitation to tell about some religious experience in their life. Asking for testimony seemed to be a code for getting folks to emote – to give expression to some pent up emotion involving the Lord.

Many times testimonials were contagious; the testimony of one would cause one of the devout to suddenly yell out, "Praise the Lord" or "Hallelujah" or some other outburst. As often as not, this would promote an emotional outpouring from someone else and pretty soon the entire church was in an uproar with Hallelujahs, Sweet Jesuses, and Glory, Glories. The minister would encourage these emotional outbursts and exclaim that The Holy Spirit had descended on our church. "The Holy Spirit is here among us! Can't you feel it? He is here! Praise the Lord!" he would say as he looked about the church as if something or somebody was about to appear.

When these sessions in the church happened, I didn't know what to expect. The Holy Spirit sounded like a ghost to me and I didn't think I wanted any part of it. I would look around the church to see if someone or something was there. It was scary. The organist would take the minister's words as her cue and begin playing some old-time spiritual like "Rock of Ages." The minister would then invite people to the altar 'to come to Jesus' and confess their sins and be saved. Invariably, the most devout of the congregation would march up to the altar and a period of loud praying, crying, moaning and a few more Hallelujahs would come from the altar rail. The most devout, like Grandma, always sat near the front so they could make it to the altar rail in nothing flat. During these sessions, I always shriveled down in the back of the church, hoping no one would notice me.

Sin was big in the 1950's and our church, not to be outdone by anyone, was one of the foremost in getting persons to admit they had sinned. As a little kid, I didn't know if I had sinned or not, even if the minister and Sunday school teachers were telling me that I had. I didn't like the moaning and yelling and the sight of grown men and women crying and pacing about the church in some sort of emotional trance. Fortunately, the Holy Spirit didn't visit too often. No one ever talked about the periodic strange happenings and since I had to attend Sunday school with the rest of the family every Sunday, I just tried to forget about those occasions. It was always a relief to get home and change out of my Sunday clothes.

The biggest meal of the week was our Sunday dinner after church. The dinner often featured one of Grandma's fried chickens and it always included mashed potatoes, with a big daub of butter melting on top of the creamy, white spuds. The meal had a southern style and flavor with plenty of bacon grease or lard and generous quantities of sugar added to many of the dishes. Vegetables often included bacon or bits of ham or, failing that, a generous helping of butter. Many times vegetables were served as a part of something else so as to make them especially tasty. Corn fritters were one of my favorites. Of course the meals featured desserts that were generally made from one or the other of the fruits or berries that we harvested. On rare occasions desert was homemade ice cream that was turned by hand.

After Sunday dinner we often went to visit another family, my cousins, unless they came to our house before we could travel to theirs. My mom and her sister were close in age and temperament and so our two families visited regularly. Visiting relatives was our chief form of family entertainment besides listening to our favorite shows on the radio. Mom's sister was Martha Moser and their family lived in Berne, Indiana. Visiting them in Berne sometimes included a stop at one of the Amish farms to buy fresh eggs if Grandma's chickens weren't laying just then. In traveling along the road to Berne we nearly always came upon one or more of the black Amish buggies clip-clopping along the paved road with their load of children and adults bundled up in their dark blue duds. Most times they would wave and we would wave back.

My Berne cousins provided playmates for me and Jim and later for my new sister also. Martha had a passel of children who were almost the same ages as us and so we played together all afternoon on Sundays. Sometimes, in the summertime some of the cousins would stay at our house for a few days or Jim or I would stay at theirs. My cousin-buddy was Butch who was one year older than me. His younger brothers were Kenny and Darry. One of our favorite pastimes was playing cowboys and Indians although Butch and I generally didn't like having the little kids play with us bigger kids. The family lived across the street from a manufacturer of concrete sewer pipes and we had great fun as cowboys and Indians in and around the giant pipes. As near as I can recall, none of the pipes ever fell despite our climbing on them.

Cowboy movies were big in the 1950's and every little kid in America wanted to be like Roy Rogers or Gene Autry with their big white hats and fancy six guns. Butch was especially taken by the cowboy movies and so he always wanted to be the cowboy. Since he was bigger and older than me, he mostly got to be the one with the six-gun while I was the lowly Indian. One Sunday afternoon as we were playing he told me he had something to show me. First, he said, he had to swear me to secrecy. He made me stick up my hand and swear I wouldn't tell and then he shoved his hand deep in his pocket and produced a shiny metal badge with a pin on the back – a real Sheriff's badge! He wouldn't say how or where he got it so I figured I better keep my mouth shut also. I never saw the badge again after that time but I am sure he kept it hidden somewhere. He died recently and I didn't get to ask him about the badge.

Butch's Dad was sort of a collector and his hobby was buying and selling. He always had all manner of stuff around the house or in the yard that he had just bought or was getting ready to sell. One of the items he bought was a 12-gage shotgun even though he wasn't a hunter. He kept it in the house. Kenny and Darry played together and they learned, like the rest of us, to play cowboys and Indians even though Darry was a little guy, the baby of the family. One day Kenny picked up the shotgun and trained it on Darry just like Roy did when he encountered an outlaw Indian. Kenny pulled the trigger. The blast must have reverberated throughout the entire house and neighborhood as Darry was instantly slaughtered by the powerful shell. I never learned any other details. Mom and Dad didn't tell us about the tragedy for awhile and Butch never talked about it so I didn't ask. Many years later I heard Martha say that she and her husband were anxious to see Darry in heaven.

Chapter 6

A New School

Central School
(built in 1910 and rebuilt 1938 after a fire)

Old Mrs. Bender must have felt sorry for me because she passed me on to the fifth grade. Since Park School only included grades kindergarten through four, getting promoted meant moving on to the grand Central School that housed grades five through eight for those of us that came from the smaller elementary schools like Park School. The imposing Central School was built in 1910 with the ever popular red brick. At my first visit, the three story building with its 57 floor-to-ceiling windows facing the front was an imposing sight for a 5th grader like me who was used to a small elementary school. Central was home to all the 5th graders in the Bluffton schools so it meant that I had some brand-new school mates.

Central School was in the west end of town so the daily walk to school changed from three blocks to more than a dozen. Since it was so far, most days I didn't walk home for lunch. When it was warm enough, we rode our bikes. In the winter we walked, unless of course, we could hop a car during the winter if the streets were snow covered. [Hopping a car meant sneaking up to the vehicle while it was stopped for some reason and grasping the rear bumper while crouched low enough that the driver couldn't see you. Then, when the car accelerated, you hung on to the bumper and let the vehicle pull you using your shoes or boots as a sort of ski. Not a recommended practice for today. For some reason, I don't remember any of us getting hurt while hopping cars.]

One of the good parts about going to Central was that suddenly, there were a lot more girls to ogle at. For some reason, 5th grade girls were a lot different than the little 4th grade girls. I never could put my finger on the reason why, but they were definitely more of an attraction for me and the other boys in my class. One of my friends from Park School whose dad owned the coal yard, Bob Purkhizer, was the first to tip me off about 5th grade girls. In fact, he told me that he had six girlfriends in 5th grade. I suspect that was right as Bob always liked sports and girls, in that order. Even with a long walk home for lunch, Bob found a little time to practice basketball during the lunch break.

Bob Purkhizer became a locally famous basketball player, dazzling fans of Indiana high school basketball with his feats as a scorer. Bob was one of the early practitioners of the newly developed jump shot enabling him to shoot over opponent's outstretched hands. He used his jump shot pretty much all the time, any time, from all positions on the court. He was heavily recruited from high school and he went on to become a starter and Purdue's leading scorer for several seasons and one of the top scorers in the Big Ten. After college, Bob tried professional basketball but he was unable to crack the big leagues in the USA so he moved to France where he became a player/coach of a professional team until his untimely death in an automobile

accident. Bob and I were big pals for a couple summers after 5th grade. He lived just two streets from my house so it was easy to get together. Bob's dad was an outdoor enthusiast and so Bob naturally followed those inclinations while I was more of a tag-along, having had

Bob Purkhizer at Purdue University

no adult encouragement or training for hunting or fishing. We fished together in the Wabash River and I went along with him a time or two in his squirrel hunting expeditions. Bob enjoyed the outings but he always seemed driven to succeed and set some record in his pursuit. For example, he always kept track of his

53

results and he wasn't shy in announcing that he shot 28 squirrels one fall season.

Bob didn't like being bested at anything, including fishing. On one occasion I caught the biggest fish, an 18 inch Channel Catfish and the biggest one I had ever seen. Bob told others in a disparaging tone that I caught the fish on a Dime Store pole (he was blanked with his expensive rod). I ignored the remark and brought the fish home to eat. On another occasion Bob established a trotline across the river and asked me for help in checking the line and to remove any of the caught fish. He said we had to do it early and how about 6:30 AM tomorrow morning? OK, I said.

The next morning I awoke early for our expedition to the river. I looked at the kitchen clock, 6:00 AM, it said. I decided to check with Bob to assure that our trip to the river was still on so I dialed his number on the big black phone. After several rings and no answer I hung up. I ate my breakfast and decided to head to his house assuming he was as good as his word. It was 6:30 AM when I knocked lightly at the back door of their house. I was let in by his mother who was wearing a housecoat. She gave me a suspicious look.

" Do you know why we are all up at this un-Godly hour? Somebody called us on the phone early this morning, waking us all up. I wish I knew who it was," she said, as she bustled about the kitchen. I wondered aloud who could have done such a fool thing. Bob and I left for the river as soon as we could thereafter.

Bob had carefully planned out his sports career with an eye to becoming one of the most lauded athletes ever in Bluffton history. He had it all planned, how he would win a varsity letter in each sport starting in 9th grade. He knew well in advance how many letters he had to win to receive the top honors and he was aiming for the highest, The Circle B Blanket. The Blanket, emblazoned with the varsity letter 'B' for Bluffton, was given to those very few athletes who had managed to win the requisite high number of varsity letters. Bob decided to forego football but play on virtually every other sport that attracted a fan following and offered a varsity letter for the top performers. Tennis was one of those sports.

Bob and I played together on the Bluffton High School Tennis Team during our Freshman year in high school. It happened that during the final match of the season he and I were playing doubles together. Bob had calculated, and he let it be known, that we needed to win our doubles match for him to win his letter in tennis that year. Further, he had determined, it was essential that he win the tennis letter to assure winning the Circle B award some four years hence.

We started the match well enough but soon our older, more experienced opponents began to win games and pull in the lead. Purkhizer was upset and I could sense his growing frustration. I was terrified that I might be the cause of him loosing his varsity letter in tennis. I gritted my teeth and decided to change my serve to a more conservative, safer stroke. The coach, watching from the sideline, yelled out his objection and I changed back to my regular serve. It didn't help. I was a pretty good tennis player, but not that good. We lost. Purkhizer, to his credit, never said anything but I felt the loss deeply. I didn't know it at the time, but that turned out to be the last tennis that I ever played with Purhizer as I ended my tennis career and began working after school during the rest of my high school days.

During and after 5th grade, clothing styles started to become more important and I think it had something to do with girls and dances. Girls seemed to like saddle shoes, those with white toes and heels but brown 'saddles' around the part that you laced up. These, coupled with bulky white socks rolled down, formed the bottom part of a popular dance outfit that featured a Poodle Skirt, so-named because an appliquéd poodle often decorated the knee length flannel skirt. The ensemble was completed with a white blouse or a sweater of bulky yarn. Favored hair styles for the girls were Pony Tails or buns of one sort or another.

Boys had a favored costume as well and a large part of it was the required shoes: white bucks, a soft suede leather shoe that was dyed white with 'spongy' soft soles. Boys wore short sleeve shirts or the popular 'T' shirts in the summer and most favored a 'flattop' haircut: an inch long cut teased to stand straight up with appropriate gobs of grease that was never admitted. I liked Brylcreem for my flattop.

This precisely defined attire was practically required for attending a school dance where the boys would stand on one side of the room watching the girls on the other. All the girls could dance and practically none of the boys. I was one of those who couldn't dance. I was also too shy to ask for help in learning how to dance until a couple years ago. So, my time at the dances was mostly agony; wishing I knew how to dance, or, for that matter, talk to girls. I can't recall that I ever mastered either skill although I went to the dances anyway, mostly to practice my olging skills as I whispered to other boys who seemed to be in the same boat as me. If you need a better understanding of this scene, picture a male dog with a long tongue, drooling, who howls at the females in heat who are safely locked in their fenced yards.

In the summertime, our community sponsored sock hops on the tennis courts. (A Sock Hop was the name for a dance. Theoretically, people who attended sock hops danced in their stocking feet – I don't know why.) Of course, no one danced in their socks on the tennis courts. Instead, we wore our white bucks if we were seriously cool or our black canvas tennis shoes with the white rubber soles. The tennis courts in my end of town were just one block from my house if I cut through Ida Moser's yard. I always knew when the sock hop started as I could hear the Disc Jockey playing the recorded music from my house. The music floated over the courts in the fading daylight on the warm summer evenings.

The dance always included music from the most popular singers of the time, Elvis Presley or Pat Boone. (Interestingly, Pat Boone was a descendent of Daniel Boone). For my birthday, Mom and Dad had given me my own record player, although I had to share it with my brother. I could barely believe I had received such an extravagant gift that included two records! My record player was a portable – a small cardboard covered, box-shaped affair with a hinged lid and the black power cord streaming from the corner like a dog's tail. The table of the record player was designed to play only the new 45 rpm records, none of the old-fashioned 78 rpm records for me. I played those two records about a 100 times the first week that I received the record player. One of the records was Elvis's *Hound Dog* and the other was something in French that had words *"Chancee da blu, da ta da ta da……..."* I memorized the words from both songs before the first week was out.

The dances on the tennis courts were not without some controversy. The Disc Jockeys hired for the dance were in reality, high school boys who had their own record collections and were willing to use them for a dance. It turned out that some of the nearby residents who could hear the music objected to some of the tunes the high school youngsters played. My neighbor, Ida Moser, was one of the complainers. She didn't think it appropriate for youngsters to be dancing to Pat Boone music that was, or should have been, in her opinion, a religious piece confined to the church –whew boy!

Around the 5th grade my summers got a little busier as I started mowing lawns in addition to my newspapering (see chapter 7). I only mowed two or three neighbor's lawns so it wasn't a big deal until I met Mrs. Simmons of Main Street (name changed to protect Mrs. Simmons). Mrs. Simmons was one of my customers on my newspaper route and one day she asked me out of the blue if I was interested in mowing her lawn for hire. "Of course," I said and we quickly agreed on a price. My friend Ted Bailey tried to warn me off the mowing job for Mrs. Simmons but I didn't take the hint and so began a long relationship of convenience for Mrs. Simmons. It turned out she wanted something more than just mowing her lawn.

Bluffton had any number of wonderful large homes that had been built in the bygone days when Wells County was young and oil was discovered. The large Romanesque style homes fronted the two most important streets in town: Main Street and Market Street. The big boss of the newspaper, Roger Swaim, lived on Market Street. Many of the largest homes were built in the late 1800's, around the same time as the County Courthouse.

M

The 1882 Studebaker House now houses the Wells County Historical Society (on Market St.)

Mrs. Simmons' house was a larger, two story home, nicer than most, like many of the houses along Main Street. Her lot and lawn was identical to others in town; 50 feet wide, 150 feet long and separated from her neighbors in the back by an alley. Her garage was at the back of her lot, adjacent to the alley. The only different thing about her lawn and most others was that her property was on a cross street as well as Main Street so she had a porch and an entrance on the side of her house that faced the cross street.

I worked for Mrs. Simmons for several years. At first, she was happy just to have me mow her lawn. It was a pretty easy job since she let me use her mower so I didn't have to push mine all the way from home just to do her lawn. After I had mowed her lawn and delivered her newspaper for some time she asked if I would mind doing a few other jobs, at the same pay, of course.

The first job beyond mowing was to trim her overgrown hedge along the alley. It hadn't been trimmed in several years so it was a big job the first time I trimmed it. After that, trimming the hedge on a regular basis became another of my services for her. Next, she asked me to dig an edge all along her sidewalk so the grass wouldn't grow over the edge and it would look neat. OK, I said.

As I got older, in addition to mowing her lawn she began asking for another service that was of a more personal nature. I felt a little uneasy about it since it seemed to be a private matter and of some significant consequence should I happen to error in the delivery of said service. The matter was resolved when I began working on a full-time basis and no longer had time to provide the service she wanted. I was relieved to be finished with the mowing and other things as well.

Oh, the personal service she wanted – it was delivering her bond and dividend checks to the bank when she received them in the mail. She didn't like going to the bank with all that money so she entrusted it to me, an eighth grader.

Chapter 7

Newspapering

I could hardly wait to get to be nine years old. According to my family, when you were nine, that meant you could put your name in at the newspaper office to be on a list for getting to be a paperboy – a real, honest-to-God, paperboy peddling about the most important newspaper in the whole country, The Bluffton News-Banner. All the big kids that I admired were paperboys and I was determined to go to work, have my own money and travel about the town with my papers. As soon as I could, I marched myself up to the newspaper office on Market Street, in the heart of town.

I was a little shy and the idea of visiting the most important office in town made me a little nervous. Nevertheless, I worked up my courage and opened the heavy door to the newspaper office. I told the lady at the counter I wanted to be a paperboy. She directed me to the man in charge of circulation. Oh, no! I have to submit to an examination, I thought as I walked nervously to the office next door where the Circulation Manager worked. He looked up as I walked in.

"Can I put my name on the list to be a paperboy?" I asked in a tremulous voice.

"Just a minute until I find the form, " he said, as he began searching his big desk. I waited anxiously, my entire future in the hands of the man bent over his desk. He asked for my name and then my address. I began to relax; maybe this was no big deal, after all.

"What's your phone number," he asked, not looking up from the paper.

"Uh, we don't have a phone," I said.

The manager seemed taken aback. "Most of our paperboys have a phone...ah, in case there is a missed paper," he said. There it was, the killer, the end of my glorious ambition to become a paperboy. I would forever be a failure while the other kids would be riding their bikes around town, passing out papers and getting rich. I returned home in a mood much glummer than when I had left.

My parents had grown up during The Great Depression and both had learned their lessons about financial management extremely well, especially my mother, who was pained if she had to throw something away. In fact, she almost never threw anything away if there was the remotest possibility that it might be useful someday. She used a leaky coffee pot for years while a new one sat unused in her cupboard. I always maintained that I failed 4th grade music try-outs because I had to use a hand-me-down Tonette with a chipped mouthpiece. Thus it was that my family didn't have a home phone until some years after everyone else.

I reported my interview results at home and the business about the phone. No one said a word so I was surprised some while later when a new telephone seemed to magically appear in our dining room. It was a party line phone, the kind that was shared by two or three other neighbors so you could listen to their calls and they could listen to yours if they wanted. Our ring was 3 short rings to distinguish a call to our house from one intended for one of the others on our party line. The telephone was a large black desk model that sat on our new television. Each time you picked up the earpiece, the telephone operator on the other end of the line would answer and say, "Number please?" After you gave a three digit number she would connect your line to whomever you were calling.

Before the new phone came I had pretty nearly given up the idea of becoming a paperboy. Then, one day, my schoolmate and friend Ted Bailey got a route. He asked if I wanted to be his assistant and I said YES, I DO and so my newspaper career began as an assistant paperboy.

One of the perquisites of being a paperboy and assistant paperboy was the newspaper bag. It was a coarse, white canvas bag with a broad shoulder strap and it had the words "**NEWS - BANNER**" prominently displayed in a colorful old English script. Once you slipped the bag over your shoulder you felt like you were in the middle of New York City ready to call out "Extra, Extra!" just like they did in the movies. Each of us got our own bag, courtesy of the News Banner. I proudly carried my bag home and hung it on the hall tree where everyone who came in the door could see it.

The News-Banner was published six times per week, after school during the week and around noon on Saturday. The newspaper boys picked up their papers for delivery in their own little room at the newspaper office. It was a concrete block building added to the side of the newspaper office and it was sparsely furnished with a couple large cabinets that 14 to 16 boys impatiently sat on while waiting for their papers. Suddenly, a chest-high, small wooden door opened in the wall and the roar of the newspaper press filled the room. The man at the window began handing out papers as they came off the press, the required number for each boy depending upon the size of his route. I helped Ted pick up his papers and we stuffed them in our bags, ready for the walk to the start of the route. I quickly learned that my notion of carefree riding my bike around town with a lightweight bag of newspaper was a small error. The papers, 136 of them for Ted's route, were heavy. We walked...and walked...and walked. First we walked uptown to pick up the papers, then we walked to the start of his route some blocks distant, then we walked the route, and then we each walked home.

The routes in Bluffton were divided so that each route had something over 100 customers. The routes were organized so that they began at the point on the route closest to town and then radiated outward from there. The town's population was around 7,000 persons and most folks subscribed to the newspaper. The town was roughly divided into an east and west side with the north –south dividing street being the main street in town and it was named, you guessed it, Main Street. The west side of town was larger; streets on the east side were 5-7 blocks long while those on the west side were double that. Most of the paper routes covered at least three streets so the paperboy walked on the order of 15 to 25 blocks on his route if he had his assistant helping. If he passed his papers without help, then his walk was approximately doubled as he had to go back and forth across the streets.

Our practice was to fold each paper into a rolled-up shape that was suitable for tossing so each could be flipped onto a customer's porch as we walked by. The route took longer to complete if the weather was inclement for on those days we put the papers behind their doors. Friday was collection day so it was also a longer day. On Saturday, before we picked up the day's edition, we went to the newspaper office to pay for our week's worth of papers out of the proceeds from our collections. Our wages were the excess from the collection, something less than $5 per week for most routes.

I got used to being an assistant paperboy helping my friend Ted Bailey and I liked having my own cash. On hot days, Ted and I would often stop in town after picking up the papers and buy ourselves an ice cream cone. I mostly got the 5¢ cone but Ted, being the boss, would buy himself the 10¢ double dip cone. On Saturdays, Ted and I would occasionally splurge and get our shoes shined at the downtown shoe shop where there was a shoe shine boy.

One day after passing papers with Ted, I got a telephone call at home. It was the News-Banner and they said they needed another paperboy and was I interested? It was a route in the west end of town, one of the less-preferred routes that ventured to the outskirts of town where there were fewer houses. "It doesn't matter to me," I told them and "YES, I AM READY TO BE A PAPERBOY." I had finally made the big time and I was happy. Soon, I would be rolling in the dough like some of the other boys!

Suburban sprawl had not yet been invented in the 1950's and Bluffton, like other small towns, had a sharp demarcation line between town and country. In most places the edge of town was clear; on one side of the road were houses with lawns and sidewalks and fire hydrants and garbage pick-up, and on the other side of the road were treeless fields with fences and furrows that were regularly farmed. The newspaper routes in Bluffton were all city routes (save one that I'll tell about later) with the houses sitting on 50 foot lots. Passing papers in the city meant walking from one porch to another, five to six houses per block where most residents were regular customers. Most routes could be completed in a little less than two hours on a normal day. The better routes that were closer to town could be finished in even less time on most days.

After several months with my west end paper route, I was assigned another route as a consequence of my improving seniority and satisfactory performance. The new route had a starting place closer to town and an ending place closer to home. It would take a little less time to pass my papers than my old route. I walked the new route with a swagger for several days befitting the big promotion that I had been given.

I kept at the newspaper delivery business for several years and I was assigned several different routes so I got to become intimately familiar with different sections of the town and the folks who lived there. Most of the homes in town were well-kept and most of the people were sober, hard-working folks who had a farm heritage somewhere in their not-too-distant past. The influence of a German heritage in town was clear given the number of German surnames on many of the routes. In addition, there were some folks who had clearly moved to Bluffton from the south. Their slow speech pattern and accent were immediately identifiable. Many folks called them 'hillbillies,' in recognition of their former homes in the hills of Kentucky or elsewhere and in marked contrast to the terrain of northeast Indiana.

Bluffton sat in the center of Wells County – a place that consisted mostly of flat farmlands only occasionally interrupted by a few acres of trees or an infrequent stream that was edged by trees and shrubs . Any view of the countryside that was not interrupted by buildings revealed the farms were on land that was perfectly level, even flatter than a pancake. It was so flat that if your dog ran away from home you could watch him run for a day or two before it was necessary to get the car and pick him up. Naming the town "Bluffton" from Bluff-town was an exaggeration. The city sits on a slight rise along side the Wabash River. From upriver, you can see the slight elevation of 30 – 40 feet that the business district resides upon. Once in town, all evidence of a bluff is gone and views looking outward reveal only flat terrain. Apparently the author of a 1937 piece in the Bluffton Evening News-Banner had never visited the town or was guilty of extraordinary hyperbole.

The city well merits the reputation of being the most beautiful and well-kept city of the Hoosier state. It is picturesquely situated on the south bank of the far-famed Wabash River, crowning high bluffs from which it derives its name and which give it a commanding view of the surrounding country.

It is a veritable paradise, combining health, wealth, beauty, comforts and pleasures, and with its miles of finely-paved streets, handsome public buildings, many beautiful and modern residences, broad and well-kept lawns, hundreds of stately shade trees, modern disposal plant, and perfect model of cleanliness and health, the city is indeed a place of beauty and attractiveness which have won renown as the "parlor city" of the entire state.

The appellation of "Parlor City of Indiana" is traced back to the beginning of the century, possibly two years earlier, following completion of the first big contracts for street paving with modern hard surface material. A visitor to the city first applied the name.—The Bluffton Evening News-Banner, September 15, 1937 (see web page www.ci.bluffton.in.us/history.htm)

By this time my friendship with Bob Purkhizer had faded somewhat and I spent time instead with my cousin, Mike Flowers, who also lived a few blocks away. Mike liked the outdoors but his dad, like mine, had never taken the time to teach his sons about hunting or other outdoor activities. When Mike and I decided on

some outdoor adventure, neither had any real knowledge of what we were about, hence there were occasional missteps during our adventures.

Our first rabbit hunting expedition was something of a misadventure, at least for me. Somehow or other we had each talked our way into the use of a rifle for our expedition. We were careful with the guns as we tromped over a

Mike Flowers, 1961

snow covered field in search of the wily fur bearers. I made sure to set the rifle in a safe position each time I climbed a fence so that I didn't shoot myself while climbing over.

After an hour or more of tromping through the snow with no rabbits in sight, we decided to head back. Again I was careful with the rifle in climbing each fence, until the next to last one. On that one, after climbing the fence and retrieving the rifle, I stumbled and the rifle came forward and the barrel, with a mind of its own, slammed itself in my face. I must have had my mouth open because I felt a sudden inrush of cold air. I gingerly rolled my tongue around my teeth and it felt like I had knocked a giant hole in my mouth. There was a sharp spot where my front tooth used to be.

I asked Mike to take a look as I pulled back my lip. He was a little too nonchalant for me. "Yeah, you chipped it a little," he said, as he continued over the next fence. Some while later I had my front tooth capped to replace the missing half.

It was about this time that I participated in the fabled camping trip to Snake Island. Snake Island was a small island in the middle of the Wabash River, no more than seven or eight blocks from my house and just upstream from the former chicken factory near the downtown. It was an island most of the time; when the water was high each spring the island was totally submerged. The island took its name from its shape: a long skinny stretch of rocky dirt in the middle of the river, maybe 200 feet long and 30 - 40 feet wide with a dozen or more stunted trees. But it was an island, surrounded by the rushing, muddy water of the Wabash River and we were going to be alone on the island fixing our meals and roughing it.

Mike said he was going to fix our supper. "Stew," he said, as he opened the container with the fixin's. I asked him where he had learned to fix stew over a campfire. "Ah, it's easy," he said, "all you need is hamburger, potatoes and carrots and catsup, lots of catsup." I probably had even less experience than Mike in cooking so it sounded good to me. I didn't ask what would keep the mess from sticking in the pan or how we were going to peel the carrots or any of that stuff. I decided those were details and we would figure out something. It was getting dark before we had the tent set up and the campfire going to cook our dinner. Just to be on the safe side, we had piled rocks all around the campfire to shield us from any errant sparks and maybe to help prevent a forest fire – probably an unnecessary precaution since we were surrounded by water.

We had managed to find plenty of wood for our campfire and so we had a pretty good fire going for dinner. Mike took on the cooking chore while I tidied up our campsite. After what seemed an eternity he announced that our dinner was ready and we seated ourselves on some of the rocks that were beginning to get quite warm.

We decided to forego using plates and so we put the frying pan between us and began to tackle the food with our forks. Tackle is the correct word. The catsup had formed a sort of glue that helped secure the top layer of food to that below. The food on the bottom of the pan was charred in place and the whole mass was one solid piece, immoveable with a simple stab of the fork. I didn't say anything as I reached for my Boy Scout knife. After sawing with the knife, I was able to dislodge a small piece of Mike's stew. I popped it in my mouth. After several minutes of determined chewing I opened my mouth. "Tastes pretty good," I mumbled before trying to swallow a big chunk.

It took a long while to get our dinner down. Neither of us said much but I suspect Mike felt a little guilty about the whole thing although it wasn't his way to admit the dinner was a failure. The best he could manage was an admission that maybe he should have used a little more catsup. We decided to sit and enjoy the campfire. I loaded some more firewood on the blaze and Mike opened another pop, the last of the batch that was supposed to serve us the entire trip.

I think I was getting my bedroll ready some while later when we heard the first loud noise like POP! It sounded like a rifle firing. We looked around. It was dark, there was no one around, and there was no reason for a loud pop. It definitely sounded like a rifle. No sooner had we sat back down when POP! Another one, only this time it seemed closer, a lot closer. POP! I thought I saw something move. There was definitely movement by the fire. It was like a bullet hitting our campsite.

We didn't know what to do so we just stood there. I was a little nervous and I wondered if it would be better to get in the tent, as if a tent could stop a bullet headed our way. Another pop, only this time one of the rocks around the fire moved, it actually moved. We bent over to examine the rock. It was hot, steaming, in fact. While we were examining it another rock popped and moved. It also was steaming. We puzzled over the fact that we had chosen probably the only place in the world to camp where rocks steamed, jumped and popped.

After one of the popping rocks had cooled, we looked at it closely. It was river rock, the kind that lined the banks of the river everywhere along the Wabash. It was porous, it had water in it, and the rock was getting very hot. Ever so slowly it dawned on us that the rocks we had used to circle our fire had moisture inside that was boiling and the pressure from the steam was causing the rocks to explode.

"I had a hunch that was the cause after the first pop," I said. "Yeah, I was pretty sure it was something like that," Mike said.

We went to bed. I don't think I ever camped at Snake Island again. I certainly never used river rock around a fire again.

Chapter 8

The Tomato & The Fair

It never occurred to me as a youngster growing up that all the faces in school and on my paper route looked just like mine. In fact, the only non-white faces I had ever seen were in the movies and they were never the main actors, only a limited sideshow. In the cowboy movies especially, there were a few Indians, an occasional Black man, (he was probably shining someone's boots) and in some movies, an outlaw band of Mexicans ravaging the southwest. One day, while I was passing my papers I was in for a big surprise. I saw a large group of Mexicans at the edge of town. Whatever were they doing near our town?

By the 1950's farmers around Bluffton had learned about the profitability of growing tomatoes for market. When I looked south and west from the edge of town on my paper route, I could see acres and acres of tomatoes. At that time, mechanized picking of tomatoes was impossible – the fragile fruits were too soft to be handled by anything other than human hands. The only thing for it was the terrible burden of inspecting the orbs for ripeness and then manually separating each fruit from its vine. Wells County farmers quickly learned that if hard, tedious labor at low cost was needed to make a substantial profit, there were none better than Mexicans to bear the burden.

As I looked outward from my vantage point along the road separating town from country, I could see that along the edge of one road, but in the field, there stood a half dozen or more small, white clapboard cabins in a row. Each had a few steps leading to a single front door with an adjacent window and another window on one wall. Nothing else adorned the plain white cabins other than black tarpaper that served as roofing material. These were cabins for migrant workers, Mexicans, who came yearly to pick tomatoes. The cabins were used for nothing else but for the Mexicans, and, judging by what I saw, they were so small that the migrant workers could use them for sleeping only.

On the several occasions that I saw the Mexican pickers they were always outdoors: children, grandmas and grandpas and parents, often scattered around an assemblage of old cars and trucks. Bluffton area farmers did little to ease the burden of the pickers. The cabins were tiny, sitting in the hot sun and they must have offered little respite for those who spent all day bent over with temperatures and humidity at equal levels on most days and tending toward hot and really hot.

The Mexicans employed their entire families to assist in the picking. They went up and down the rows filling bushel baskets with ripe tomatoes until one of the adults carried the heavy basket to a nearby truck. From there, the farmer or one of his white hired hands took over. He drove the truck to the Bluffton canning factory where the tomatoes were inspected, graded, sorted and then washed and processed for canning. Bluffton tomatoes were shipped all over the U.S. in cans bearing a variety of labels. It was a profitable operation benefitting the farmers, the factory managers and owners, and the several

Bluffton residents who worked at the canning factory during the harvest period.

The Mexicans picked the tomatoes and then left. I don't recall that the Bluffton community ever had any events or made any special provisions to acknowledge or celebrate the essential, hard work of the migrant workers who helped enrich the farmers and the community. The workers endured their hardships, collected their wages, and then left to pick something else, somewhere else. Their lives in the Bluffton late summer and fall must have been a mindless struggle for the brief period that our lives and theirs intersected.

The other minority group in the United States, African-Americans, was not present in Bluffton during this period. Black Americans had begun their migration from the Deep South shortly after the turn of the century in response to the growing need for labor in the northern cities. In January of 1914, Henry Ford's famous call for men at a wage of $5 per day prompted a flow of north-bound Blacks who had never dreamed they could earn that much money. The migration to the North was further promoted after World War II when black soldiers heard about opportunities in the North from their fellow white soldiers. By the mid 1950's Civil Rights unrest in the South had reached epidemic proportions with Rosa Parks and Dr. Martin Luther King helping Blacks. White reaction to these efforts prompted many Blacks to leave their homes in the dead of night and head for cities in the north.

It was surprising there were no black African-Americans in Bluffton in the 1950's since there were lots in the big city of Fort Wayne only 25 miles distant. I never heard of any suitable reason why Blacks were not In Bluffton other than a vague rumor about a former ordinance, but it is likely that they knew they were unwelcome. Sadly, Bluffton was the site of at least one Ku Klux Klan demonstration and there may have been others held secretly. It is likely that whites who had emigrated to Bluffton in earlier times from the southern states were responsible for this attitude. It would be inaccurate to say that people living in Bluffton were not prejudiced in the 1950's.

In contrast to the treatment accorded minorities, others in Bluffton celebrated the fall harvest in a big way. Many in the community were involved in planning and organizing an event known everywhere as The Bluffton Street Fair. The event was so named because the fair occupied the downtown business district and the streets were closed for the week of the fair. It began in 1898 and by the time I knew about it, it was a well-organized operation controlled by a committee of city fathers. The Fair Committee began planning the next year's hoopla immediately following the close of the prior fair. The free Street Fair (no cost to attend) was a combination harvest festival, carnival, marketing enterprise, celebration of homemaking and gardening skills, and a chance for farmers to show off their horses, pigs and other animals. The Street Fair Committee controlled a substantial budget and they used it wisely to provide free entertainment during the fair to attract visitors. The consequence of all the planning and work by the blue ribbon Committee ensured a successful fair year after year with attendance by folks from all around the area.

The carnival rides and the games of chance were the big attractions for a kid like me who had just grown out of short pants and had a little pocket money to spend. And I was just the sort of customer that the flim-flam men who operated the games had in mind when they stocked their shelves with all sorts of Teddy Bears and kewpie dolls that made wonderful prizes for young boys wanting to impress young girls. The practice of boy's giving their prizes to a favorite girl was everywhere evident during The Fair as the girls carried their gifts around during the entire week of the fair. It wasn't easy winning a Teddy Bear. I learned the hard way that it would have been far cheaper to have bought one.

The other major attraction for me was the rides. The favorite rides, of course, were the scariest. The one that attracted the most attention was the hair raising, twisting, turning, noisy torpedo-type tube that you sat in before buckling up as a reminder of just how dangerous the thing was. When the contraption started suddenly you were upside down and then right side up but flying through the air and circumscribing small, bumpy circles. The ride ended as suddenly as it began. Most of us scrambled out as quickly as possible but complained to our watching friends about how short the ride was. I laughed about the ride only after I managed the entire 45 second excursion without throwing up.

The rides were 25¢ each; an expensive proposition when it was possible to ride 6 or 7 times in an hour and your available cash was a few dollars for the week. But wonder of wonders, a newspaper boy like me had a distinct advantage over my friends. Our boss of bosses, Roger Swaim, the majority owner, editor and publisher of the News-Banner gave each paperboy 30 free ride tickets -30 tickets! I had never seen that many of the valuable ducats in one place. I couldn't imagine they were to be all mine. My respect for Mr. Swaim jumped about 20 points after he passed out the tickets.

The Street Fair had an appeal for nearly everyone. The attraction on Tuesday evening was the 7: 00 PM official opening after the parade through the mid-way. The parade featured the officials of the fair, The Bluffton Street Fair Band, floats prepared by many organizations and the festooned horses and other animals marching head to tail along the route.

The free acts were a major draw for audience. All manner of professional acts, and a few amateur ones, performed throughout the week at elevated stages set up around the midway. Each time an act was ready to perform, the Street Fair Band with their drums banging and horns blowing would lead a parade to the appropriate stage. In the absence of television, the stage acts were a special treat for the farmers and small town folks who had never witnessed performers of this caliber. Some of the free act performers were dare-devils who performed feats of wonder for an appreciative audience. There were wire-walkers and aerialists of one sort or another performing high above the mid-way, some with free standing platforms, and an occasional dare-devil who performed from wires attached to the tallest part of the 1889 sandstone court house that stood proudly in the center of town.

Like most Bluffton residents, our family was an enthusiastic supporter of the fair. My Grandfather Jesse has been a member of the Fair Committee and all of us thereafter naturally attended most fair events, except my Grandmother Nellie. According to the Wesleyan Church, the fair was too secular and there were too many activities that were questionable, so it was better to stay away. Grandma must have been emotionally conflicted as she snuck into the Community Building to see the gardening and homemaking projects that were entered. She and

Grandpa also attended some of the free acts but she carefully avoided the midway and its evil influences in compliance with the teachings of the church.

The church felt that one of the evils of the mid way was the Girl Show, more commonly called a burlesque show in the big cities. At the Street Fair it was just The Girl Show, and all the men and boys over 10 years old knew what it was all about. You were supposed to be 18 years old to attend the show but I never saw anyone examining any official papers if you had a dollar at the entrance. None of the youngsters my age, however, had the courage to try entering the establishment by the front entryway. Instead, all the boys talked about sneaking into the show by crawling under the tent at some area away from the entrance. I don't know if anyone was successful in trying to enter that way or not.

When I finally did attend the show some years later (through the front entrance) I enjoyed it. I remember that the show was crowded with men as we all shuffled in to find a seat on wooden benches stretched in front of a small, but high stage in front of us. The lights went out and the blackness was relieved by blue-white ultraviolet lights focused on the stage. As the audience started to grow restive, suddenly recorded music began to blast over the crowd and a single woman came on stage. The UV light focused on her bottom as she turned to reveal her backside that was covered with skin tight panties. The panties were decorated and the UV light illuminated what seemed to be a pair of hands that glowed white. Nothing else of the woman was visible save the hands which made the outline of her buttocks visible.

The dancer moved to the music and the illuminated hands moved. Then she began flexing her muscles and the hands seemed to move and twitch. That was the high point of her dance. As she danced the hands moved over her behind and the men in the audience yelled, hooted and laughed. The rest of the show featured similar acts involving women dancing to recorded music and men howling at suggestive moves. It was fun to hear the men's reaction to the dances and I didn't regret the $1 admission.

The Fair Committee watched over the Girl Show carefully since many residents felt strongly about it. It was a clear draw for many of the farmers and a clear abomination for many of the farmer's wives. The sense of the Committee about the show was that it was a necessary part of the Fair since it was a money maker for the both the Carnival operator and an audience draw for the Fair. I recall a newspaper story detailing the Fair Committee's discussion of the Girl Show. One of the members of the committee was quoted as saying, "If the girls can't be younger than 40, keep the show out of here." Apparently, at least one member of the Committee wanted to assure the show met his own preferences and quality standards although I think he was pretty fussy since forty years old seems pretty young to me now.

Chapter 9

Pranks and Comics

Finding entertainment during my years in the Middle school was never a problem. There always seemed to be plenty to do in addition to my paper route and the occasional chore that I had to do. One pleasurable pastime was going to the movie. There was one theatre in town, The Grand Theatre, and it was right downtown. After I passed my papers on Saturday it was often movie day. I could spend most of the afternoon watching the previews, the shorts (brief comedy reels) the news reels and finally the featured movie. If it was a double feature, you could spend the entire afternoon at the show for a mere 25 cents.

My second favorite pastime was comic books: buying, reading, and trading them. In the days before I had responsibility for my money, I was allowed only one or two of the ten cent comic books a week. Since I could read a comic book cover to cover in 20 minutes or so, one per week hardly quenched my appetite for the likes of Superman, Dick Tracy, and Archie & Jughead. I quickly learned the fine art of trading comics. Jim and I both shared a passion for comics but we each kept our books separate. After we had thoroughly read each other's books, our practice was to badger the neighborhood gang for trading. Only our friends the Shady boys were also avid readers and so trading with them was often fruitful. I thought they had a pretty good supply of comics till I was granted visiting rights to the comics that my cousin, Dave Flowers, owned and kept in his bedroom closet. Whoa! he had comics stacked waist deep in his closet. His were all in good shape too, not like mine that had been read 20 times and were all dog-eared. Unfortunately, Dave didn't seem too interested in trading, probably because he had already read all the ones that I owned. I managed to get only one or two from him.

Other than movies and comic books, most of our entertainment was centered on activities that we made up to amuse ourselves. Playing pranks was one of the sources of endless amusement and everyone seemed to be either a perpetrator or victim at one time or another. Halloween was a favorite time for kids to play pranks during the several days leading up to the night of Halloween. Some folks called the evening before Halloween 'Devils Night' but in the case of our gang in the south end of town it was more like Devil's Week preceding the week of Halloween. Before I recount some of the Devil's Week activities that occurred in our neighborhood, readers should understand that I am merely reporting activities that I understand took place; not that I participated in such fiendish undertakings myself.

A favorite prank around many neighborhoods was to soap windows. Soaping a window meant smearing the window with a bar of soap and, to add insult to injury, using the soap to write some sort of clever phrase or ugly swear word requiring the owner of said window to immediately wash same if they wanted to continue as a respectable citizen in a respectable neighborhood. Car windows were easy to soap. Any car left parked on the street was a candidate for soaping. House windows were a little more challenging as the risk of being caught was substantially higher. Choosing a soap that wouldn't make noise when scraped across a window was one of the tricks of the trade in the manly art of soaping. Normal practice in soaping house windows was to sneak around to the side of the house and coat the storm windows with a good coating of soap, enough so that the home occupants would be sure to see it on first glance. Soaping a front window or a front door was a soaping job involving more risk and generally attempted only by the most experienced of soapers.

Almost as common as soaping windows was the old phantom visitor trick. This prank involved knocking on someone's door and then disappearing into the shrubs or hiding around the corner before the homeowner answered the knock. This prank was only counted as complete after knocking on the same door two or three times. Teacher's homes were favorite targets for this clever prank.

One prank required a tool to rattle against a storm window in hopes of making a strange, frightening noise. The apparatus involved a wooden spool, the kind that was used to store and dispense sewing thread. You had to use your pocketknife to notch the beveled, raised end of the spool, and then slip the spool loosely over a nail so it would spin when you pulled a thread that was looped over the spool. The idea was to spin the spool against a window so that the notched wood would create a whirring sound, strange enough to frighten the inhabitants. I never heard anyone say whether this trick really worked since the perpetrators were always running off before the effects could be learned.

A variety of other pranks were developed but used less often than soaping. One of the most talked about but only rarely employed was the old burning bag trick. In its most simplified version, the clever bag man would collect the freshest dog poop available, or even better, a fresh cow pie, and insert it carefully into a large brown grocery bag. The bag would also be stuffed with a crumpled newspaper. The bag would then be strategically placed on a front stoop at a house where the lights were on and someone was sure to be home. A gang member would then pitch a burning match into the paper, knock on the door and simultaneously yell, "Fire, Fire" and then hightail it to safety. The rest of the gang would be safely hidden in a position to watch the homeowner rush to the door and attempt to stamp out the fire. The prank was complete only when the gang guffawed loudly enough for the homeowner to hear and give chase.

Each year, just before Halloween, there were also isolated cases of some really nasty pranks involving rotten eggs, spoiled tomatoes, or some other foul substance ending up on someone's house or car. This would be followed the next night with armies of freshly scrubbed children in costumes begging for treats door to door. Amazingly, those who were required to answer phantom door bells one night would be handing out candy the next, possibly to the same children. It just doesn't make sense now, but it did then.

Teachers were subject to pranks all year long. We always thought our teachers were not clever enough to catch on to some of the pranks, but now, I'm not so sure. One of the best that I recall occurred in 6th grade when we were assigned the task of writing and then reciting a poem. The teacher gave us one day to work on the assignment. One of the boys in my class, I'll call him

Gene, confided that he didn't like poems, didn't plan to write one and besides, he had a better idea.

"If she calls on me, I am going to recite my favorite one," he said, as he assumed a dramatic pose and then began after a lengthy pause.

"Here I sit, brokenhearted. Paid a nickel for a shit, and all I did was farted."

Now, every boy in our class had heard this poem recited about 1,000 times so it was not the poem that was so funny, it was the idea that he would recite it in a classroom that was outrageously hilarious. Especially a classroom where bodily functions were assumed not to exist and the foulest word ever spoken was 'darn' and people had been sent to the Principal even for that.

The next day was poem day. True to her word, teacher began calling students to recite their creations. As the afternoon wore on, many of the boys stood, recited a feeble poem about baseball or apple pie and then sat down. Gene hadn't been called and most of us boys began to relax. Then, just before 3:00 PM and school ended, teacher called out.

"Gene, what do you have for us?"

Gene rose and slowly walked to the front of the room with a sly smile on his face as he looked at several of the boys in class. A couple boys snickered out loud. I pinched myself to keep from laughing. Teacher's frown was enough to silence the snickers. Gene began, but his voice seemed to be coming out of him in slow motion. I trembled in fear for his safety as I heard the first words... 'Here I sit brokenhearted'.... Gene's voice went on in a slow monotone. I could see Gene in the Principal's office….'paid a nickel' ….the Principal with a raised switch over Gene's backside….'for a pencil'. What? He continued….'paid a nickel for a pencil but it broke before I started.' Gene sat down with a smile. All the boys gasped and laughed out loud. Teacher dismissed class immediately as the bell rang out.

Adults seemed to countenance childhood pranks even though they didn't normally participate. For example, there was the business of a chivaree, although we didn't know it by that name. The practice was for the friends of a bride and groom to engage in organized harassment of the couple on their wedding night, assuming the friends could find out where the couple was spending their first night. (I never knew anyone in those days who could afford to go on a honeymoon). I participated in two or three chivarees where we decorated the newlywed's vehicle and then attempted to follow them home to disturb their first night together. A favorite prank was having a few folks sneak away from a wedding reception to make changes to the couple's bed and bedroom like hiding sheets and blankets or other changes that the newlyweds would need to correct before bedtime. Everyone seemed to accept these pranks in good spirits and I never heard of anyone getting angry. A more likely result was a silent determination to 'get even' at a future date.

My mother was an example of adult acceptance of pranks. Normally she was too busy to engage in activities like this what with her housekeeping, sewing, cooking, canning vegetables and so forth. At least, that's the impression that she gave. I recall one morning after Dad had gone to work and we were sitting at breakfast when she told Jim and me that her brother had something to give us. What? We both wanted to know.

"A map," she said. "It came from a childhood friend that he used to know years ago."

She went on to tell the story of how her brother Alden used to play with this friend and like lots of boys they explored the countryside all around Bluffton. Once they found some arrow heads and old coins at an isolated spot near the river. Shortly after, the friend and his family moved to California and Alden never heard from him again, that is, until recently. Alden said he recently received a letter from his old friend. The letter explained that the friend was cleaning up some things and he came across the old map and he thought that maybe Alden would like it. He said that he had always intended to revisit the site and dig for whatever he could find since he thought there must be more things there than the few arrowheads and old coins they had discovered. Alden said he was too busy to go on a wild goose chase but maybe Jim and I were interested.

Arrowheads and old coins, maybe other treasures, you bet. I could see the wheels turning in Jim's brain just like my own. I wanted to skip school and head out, but wait a minute, we didn't have the map yet.

"So, when are we going to get the map?" I asked.

"Oh, yes, the map," she said vaguely. "Well, we'll see. You had better get off to school now. Oh, by the way, do you know what day it is today?" Both of us had a vacant stare.

"It's April 1st." Then a big smile came. "April Fool's Day, ha, ha, ha."

Big brother Jim got it right away. It took me half the way to school before I realized that I had been completely sucked in about the map and the treasures. It didn't seem right and I felt betrayed. Adults weren't supposed to do stuff like that, let alone parents. By the time I got to school I began plotting my revenge and I felt better.

Chapter 10

Big Changes

Sometime after my sister was born in 1950 and I was in Middle School at the big Central School, my dad finished another home improvement job: I got a new bedroom, shared of course, with Brother Jim. The new bedroom was our former attic, furnished with hardwood floors and a shiny new hardwood stairway leading up from the dining room. At one end of the bedroom was the stairway with a closet on either side, and at the other end were our twin beds, one on each side of a single large window overlooking the backyard. The bedroom with its low, slanted ceiling was a great sanctuary compared to our former quarters even though it was shared. The main disadvantage was that it got hot in the summertime.

Air conditioning was unknown in our neighborhood in the 1950's. Our upstairs bedroom with its single window had limited air circulation and the summer heat piled up in the room even with a fan whirring away at full speed. When the humidity was high in the summer time it was easy to get up early; if I slept late it meant awakening with a sweaty body and nothing to look forward to but more of the same the rest of the day. Since everyone shared the burden of the heat and humidity, no one paid much attention to complainers. I learned to keep my mouth shut.

A big change occurred in the dining room in addition to the shiny new stairway: the addition of a television and the elimination of the old Philco radio. Television was developed bit by bit over a long period but it finally became commercially viable in 1947. At first it was expensive and there was very limited programming available. In addition, the screens were small, the pictures were snowy, and only black and white pictures were available. In spite of these shortfalls, everyone wanted one, including our family. By 1954, 55% of American families owned a set and our family was one of them. The new TV in the dining room meant the loss of the old Philco radio. Gone were the shared evenings sitting around the radio with the glowing light and the sound coming through the fabric at the front of the console. Gone was the picture created by our vivid imaginations as the Thin Man chased down criminals and you could hear his footsteps on the pavement. Gone was the mind's eye picture of the Lone Ranger on his stunning white horse, Silver. Although we got our new TV, we lost the intimacy of radio and its effect on our imaginations.

In 1955, television had one of its biggest moments: Elvis was on The Ed Sullivan show. It was a major event in broadcasting and newspaper editors around the country weighed in calling Elvis and his hip gyrations a bad influence on the youngsters of America. They saw a sexual component in Elvis' performance and they warned of dire consequences if he were allowed to perform on national TV. The show went on anyway. In the event, the performance was innocent and both Elvis and Ed Sullivan profited from the show. Elvis sang *Hound Dog* and a few of his hit recordings to thunderous applause. I was an Elvis fan like most other Middle School students across the country, but I stuck with the flattop haircut instead of imitating Elvis' long black locks.

My Grandfather Jesse began to have health problems around this time and so he moved in with our family under the watchful care of my mother. [I learned later that Jesse was suffering from Alzheimer's, only then it was called hardening of the arteries.] He and I watched television together and he liked the daytime children's shows. At the end of the show when the performer waved to his imagined audience, Grandpa would wave back with a smile on his face. "I always liked that guy," he would say. I thought it was cute in a grown-up sort of way.

Grandpa Jesse had worked in stores all his life and he maintained his habit of dressing up every day. I think he only owned "Sunday clothes" as he wore dark wool trousers, a white shirt and suspenders every day. Even in the summer his heavy wool pants were carefully pressed and his black, high top shoes were polished. I remember that he spent a lot of time in our living room watching the family and letting his Lucky Strikes burn down in his fingers. He talked to me a little but I wasn't smart enough to sit down and ask about his history.

I fell into a routine at Central School and I managed to get promoted from one class to another each year so that by 7th grade things were going pretty smoothly. Then, suddenly, things were thrown into a tizzy when my mother presented the family with a new baby: a new brother for me. It struck me that I could take on the role of big brother and teach the little guy the ropes when he got bigger. For awhile, his presence was a nuisance what with the crying and his demands on MY MOM. I took solace in the fact that soon I could take him on my paper route, show him the ropes and boss him around. After a few months the novelty of having a baby brother wore off. It seemed to be taking him an awfully long time to grow up. I began to ignore his presence. Finally, he and my little sister became like one of those awful warts that I got now and then: always around, but best left alone or it could become a big pain.

My two little siblings also presented a challenge during family vacations. Our practice was to take a sightseeing vacation each summer. We would make arrangements for someone to take over the paper routes (Brother Jim also had a paper route) and then pile into the family car for a week-long trip to somewhere. The car was packed – four kids, cardboard suitcases and various bags of all sorts including some groceries to reduce restaurant costs- all jammed in a 1953 blue Chevrolet. Dad did all the driving and we traveled as long as possible on the first day to reduce lodging costs. The first summer that we traveled with the new baby was a trip to The Smoky Mountains, Ruby Falls, Mammoth Cave, and Lookout Mountain. We stayed at a motel high up in the Smokies at a picturesque spot adjacent to a rushing stream. After unpacking the car, Dad and I wandered to the stream while Mom took care of the baby.

It was a neat spot. In a few minutes, both the old man and I were at the river's edge, eyeing the boulders and rocks scattered along and across the river. I couldn't resist the urge to try out my sure-footedness by springing from one boulder to another. The old man was right behind. He liked doing kid stuff and he was as risky as I was like the time we went sliding on the ice and he fell and cracked two ribs.

I leapt from rock to rock. I was surprised at how noisy the stream was as I ventured almost to the center of the shallow stream on top of one particularly large boulder. There it was! I could see a path from one rock to another all the way across the river. If I can only get past this next little rock, I thought. Splash!

The rock rolled and I had one foot in the water. The speed of the current made me lose my balance and splash! The other foot went in the water on the slippery rocks, so slippery that I couldn't keep my balance. And suddenly I was on my hands and knees. The water was very cold. I tried to stand and the current pushed me over. The next thing I knew there was water up to my neck as I rolled over again, barely feeling the smooth, slippery rocks under my hands and knees. Again I tried to stand and again the rush of the water was trying to turn me over. As I pushed up, suddenly the strong arm of my dad lifted me up. He was standing in the cold water right next to me. We waded to the shore, avoiding all the big rocks and walking gingerly on the polished, smooth rocks in the water. At the shore he asked if I was alright. Just then, he seemed like a pretty good guy, not like the old man that grumbled sometimes.

The rest of the vacation went pretty much according to schedule and we saw all the sights without problems. One of my favorite spots was Mammoth Cave but it was a little scary when they turned the lights off for several seconds so we could get used to total darkness. I liked the cave but I wasn't too fond of somebody's idea to turn out the lights while I was a mile or two underground. When we got back to the car after seeing the cave we found that someone had pasted a large colorful poster on the bumper. It said 'Mammoth Cave' and it really stuck out all by itself on the shiny chrome bumper. My dad didn't like the sticker. I could tell he didn't by the colorful swear words when he tried, without success, to peel it off.

After Mammoth Cave it was back in the car with its load of candy bar wrappers, dirty diapers and fussy children (except me, of course) and then off to the next sight. We were amazed at

Look-Out Mountain and my dad was again irked by the mysterious appearance of another bumper sticker. It also resisted removal even with additional swearing including some that I had never heard before. By the time we got home from vacation our car had been plastered with stickers: "See Rock City," "See Ruby Falls" and "Look-Out Mountain." The 1953 Chevrolet Belaire was never the same after that trip.

As the 8th grade drew to a close, one of the biggest, scariest things in my life loomed ahead; the dreaded move toward High School. It wasn't High School itself that was the problem, it was the dreaded *initiation.* The deal was that High School upperclassmen prowled around town looking for kids that were going to be 9th graders. Any kid found wandering the streets was fair game for High School *initiation.* Every graduating 8th grade boy knew the risk; being kidnapped and subjected to some form of humiliation or torture at the hands of an upperclassman; razing, some people called it and every 8th grader was on the look-out for an upperclassman.

I didn't know too much about the practice even though Brother Jim was an upperclassman. I don't think he knew too much about it himself. Anyway, the risk was the sort that was in your mouth; you could taste it especially when you were out about town alone. For me, that was most of the time what with my paper route and all. Of course, you didn't talk to anyone about it, you just looked at your peers with a kind of deep understanding and hoped it would be them instead of you. I think the idea was that if you survived the razing that would mean you were ready for high school.

Two of the favorite kidnapping tricks that I heard most about was the wire walk and the long distance trek. The wire walk worked like this: you were taken to a place outside of town where there happened to be a deep ditch with a pair of wires suspended over it. The incoming freshman was required to climb on the wire and make his way across the chasm. One slip from the suspended wire meant you were toast – the upperclassmen would drive off leaving you forever in the ditch. The long distance trek was more of a test of stamina. The upperclassmen would blindfold the freshman, drive him to a secluded area outside town and dump him off, leaving him to find his way home alone.

For some reason, I was never kidnapped. I never figured out why and I was afraid to make any inquiries. Thus it was that I passed from 8th grade into high school without any particular incident. I must have slipped through the upperclassmen net like a submarine in a WWII movie; anyway, I made it so here I am writing my memoirs.

Chapter 11

High School

Bluffton High School (around 1961)

Well, I finally made it to the big time: Bluffton's P.A. Allen High School, the top educational institution in the county, the seat of higher learning, the place for the Grand Poo-bahs of the P's and Q's. Not everyone can boast of making it this far. I don't want to brag, but my Grandma and Grandpa Tudor both only made it through the 6th grade and my great uncle Fred only made it to the 3rd grade before he quit. So here I am, representing a family with educations you wouldn't want to brag about, standing at the beginning of a glorious career in I don't know what.

Yesterday I finished my freshman orientation so today I had to sign up for the classes I intend to take for the next four years. I had to choose one of the several different schedules of classes offered: General Studies, Academic, Vocational, etc. The Guidance Counselor said it was an important decision that could affect the rest of my life. He said it was like choosing a boat to travel in toward my goals in life. (I didn't mention to him that I didn't have any goals). I didn't know what to choose so I did what seemed best at the time; I asked other kids what they were taking. My cousin, Mike Flowers, said he was taking the Academic schedule. I asked why and he said because most of the prettiest girls were signing up for those classes. It sounded like a pretty good reason to me so I decided to choose that boat to go somewhere.

The Academic schedule means that I will need to study Latin, Chemistry, Algebra and lots of stuff like that. I didn't even know the school had studies like that. And teachers that knew about such things! Who would have guessed? Not me. I had always thought of Bluffton as a sleepy, backwater town with farmers who didn't know all that much. I guess the old town has made considerable progress in the last few years. Anyway, I signed up for the hard stuff in school so I guess I'll be hitting the old books sometime soon.

I was a little surprised during my first day at High School. Jim had told me all about class schedules and study hall and things like that, so that didn't bother me. What surprised me most was the parking lot. High School students driving cars to school – Whooeee! For some reason, it never entered my mind that I would be going to school with all those kids who were old enough to drive, including some who owned their own cars. They were practically adults and I would be going to school with them, maybe I would be in the same classes. Suddenly, I felt like a little snot-nosed kid again.

Cars were a frequent topic for high school boys as I was entering high school in 1957 and everyone wanted one, including me. We talked endlessly about the hottest car on the scene, the '57 Chevrolet. The car's humongous tail fins were a trend-setter. Anyone could buy one for $2,500, a fair price for that period when gasoline was a paltry $0.31 per gallon. None of the '57 Chevys were in the high school parking lot, rather, the student lot was full of 5 and 10 year old cars that had seen better days like the 1948 Plymouth that my buddy from the South End Dirty Necks, Rich Noonan, drove to school every day. Soon after I started high school, Rich picked up Jim and me and a few of the others from our South End gang for the trip to school. It was about a mile from our house as it was at the opposite end of town so Rich's car ride was a welcome change from walking or riding my bike to Central School.

Rich was a pretty good driver for a high school student and a lot better than some of the other high school drivers that I rode with on occasion. The worst of the drivers was a friend who was one year older than me who thought he was a race car driver. He careened down the streets in town without slowing and barely glanced at unmarked corners for oncoming traffic. He drove for less than a year before his driving practices caught up with him and the result was a crash. There were three of us in the car, all sitting in the front seat when he sped through an intersection and I suddenly found myself on my hands and knees in someone's front yard. The doors to the car had sprung open on an impact that I didn't see and all three of us were thrown from the car. Remarkably, no one was hurt but his old '49 Chevy coupe was banged up pretty severely. He didn't drive for awhile after that.

Some high school drivers drove carefully to protect their vehicles. The best of the lot was my buddy Ted Bailey who had a

shiny blue 1952 Chevrolet coupe. Ted must have washed his car two or three times per week since I never saw it anything less than immaculate. The pin striping and chromed wheels with the fancy wheel covers made his car stand out and he drove carefully wherever he went. I was a frequent passenger in Ted's car as we rode to school or cruised around town on weekends in search of females. One of the places

Ted Bailey

that we frequented was the town's root beer stand.

The root beer stand was a drive-in restaurant that featured root beer, the best hot dogs around, and of course, delightful root beer floats. The drive-in had speakers at each designated parking spot where the patron would push a button to speak with a clerk and place his order. The black root beer was served icy cold in large glass mugs with thick, bubbly foam on top. The drive-in was the place to see and be seen as it was easily the most popular place in town. One of the attractions was the waitresses. The owner always managed to hire the prettiest, most popular girls to serve customers. Ted and I could spend an entire weekend evening circling the drive-in several times before finally ending up with a 10¢ mug of icy cold root beer at the stand. If we had circled the root beer stand a dozen or more times during the evening, we would order a hot dog or two, slathered in mustard and onions, to make our evening complete.

I soon learned that high school offered several social opportunities for students. Two activities that I became involved with were Hi-Y and DeMolay. DeMolay was connected with the Masonic Lodge and we met weekly in their large rented room downtown, above the hardware store. I didn't last very long as a DeMolay novice, not even long enough to find out the meaning of the name [which I just discovered was in honor of Jacques DeMolay who was named Grand Master of the Knights Templar In 1298]. DeMolay seemed a little boring to me what with their homage to all the Pooh-Bahs who sat on the points of the compass. High school Hi-Y was another matter.

The Hi-Y boys were an active group in high school and I soon learned that Hi-Y was an organization somewhat like YMCA and they valued raising money for various purposes. I understood that. In our school, Hi-Y money invariably was donated to school activities like the prom or some needed item for class or school. Our group raised money by operating the concession stand at high school basketball games; an activity that generated a sizable income for an operation run by high school boys. By some peculiarity, I became the treasurer of Hi-Y so I managed the money under careful supervision of our teacher/sponsor, of course.

One of my jobs as Treasurer was to collect the money after each basketball game and put the cash box in the Principal's car trunk, locking and returning his keys thereafter. One Monday morning, after a particularly busy Friday night at the concession stand, I was called from Latin class to Principal Fred Parks' office. Fred and another teacher were alone in the office as I walked. "So," Principal Fred asked, "where is the concession stand money?" His tone seemed cold. He stared at me and I wondered if he or the teacher had the handcuffs.

"I put it in the trunk like every other time," I stammered.

"Well, it wasn't there."

The Principal looked to the other teacher while I shuffled my feet. A moment that lasted about a month passed by before Fred owned up that he, in fact, had the money that had just been given to him by the teacher in the room. I listened intently as the teacher, a man by the name of Chad Fornshell, explained that he had found the cash box in the trunk of **HIS** car that morning and delivered it to the Principal. It turned out that Fornshell and Parks had both recently purchased a new Chevrolet of the same style and color and we all three learned that the trunk key to one worked for the other's car. I had innocently put the cash box in Fornshell's car instead of Park's car that was parked nearby. Who said being Treasurer was easy! They let me go and they probably had a good laugh at my discomfiture.

One of the things that Hi-Y featured was a summer camp. One of my Hi-Y high school chums, Larry Votaw, and I had agreed to spend a week there. In the spirit of the YMCA, the camp was set up for healthy, wholesome activities for youngsters. It didn't exactly work out that way. For example, I learned to smoke my first cigarette at the camp when one of my cabin mates from another city said that he couldn't spend a whole day without a cigarette. He was a friendly guy and one thing led to another and so I tried one of the nasty things. I didn't begin smoking then, but it surely led the way to the subsequent mistake of smoking some years later, a habit I came to regret.

Larry Votaw and I had schemed several months before the Hi-Y summer camp. Larry had a car, and we planned to drive across the state to the camp site that was located in the woods in a rural area. Although the drive was a few hours at most, we planned to leave a day early, check into a hotel in the nearby town of Delphi IN, and spend the afternoon and evening prowling the area nightlife in search of adventure. Of course we couldn't tell anyone about our long hatched plan as we drove off on a late summer morning. The event pretty much worked out as we had planned although we didn't find any nightlife to speak of and nothing untoward happened during our high adventure. In fact, it was sort of a let-down when we learned that our plan was uncovered when the high school sponsor/teacher called one of our homes to remind of the summer camp and no one seemed particularly disturbed that we had already left.

In my freshman year of high school my circle of friends (mostly still boys) began to slowly change as the older members of the gang moved on to new activities. No longer was it a simple matter of going out the front door and down the block to find one or more of the gang ready for some activity. Since many of the old friends now had cars and were busy with jobs or girlfriends, some planning was needed to make a date for an activity. I had quite a few friends who were older than me since I got to know them from their association with my older brother Jim. With so many of them having their own cars, it was easy to form friendships even with those who lived some distance from my neighborhood. Where to go and what do was often the question and many times the answer was to come to my house for an hour or an evening of playing cards.

My dad liked to play cards. He enjoyed playing with anyone so when one of my friends came to our house, as likely as not, a game of euchre with my dad sitting in would break out around the kitchen table. If there was only one of my friends, Dad would convince my mother to join in as she liked to play also if she wasn't busy on one of her endless household tasks. The games were often loud, passionate affairs with lots of whoops and hollering as some unexpected card was played or someone surprised the others with consistent winning or losing. My dad liked to win and he was a competitive player so the games never lacked enthusiasm. He would often slam his discard on the table with a clenched fist to make his knuckles bang the table for emphasis. Sometimes all the players would follow his practice; to an outsider the players would have seemed like a group of intent on breaking our kitchen table.

My grandmother didn't believe in card playing since the church frowned on it as the work of the devil. Her practice was to drop in to our house through the back door for unannounced visits. We always tried to avoid a confrontation by hiding the playing cards when she came to the door. Since it was only a few steps from the back door to the kitchen, it was always a mad scramble to sweep the cards off the table and out of sight before she passed through the kitchen on her way to the living room. She must have wondered about the many times she saw me and my friends sitting around the kitchen table looking like Cheshire cats that had swallowed the bird.

I decided I liked high school. The studying wasn't too bad and the classroom tedium was often broken by some funny happening. Our Latin teacher was one whose class was often disturbed by someone's attempt at humor. After a chapter of study on Roman institutions, she once innocently asked if anyone could explain the Roman Forum. Without hesitation Mike Flowers raised his hand to answer. "The forum is the sum of two-um plus two-um," he said.

High school was also a busy time for me. In addition to school and family activities, I continued on my paper route and did other jobs like mowing and errands. Those things soon came to an end; however, when I was called for another, more important job.

Chapter 12

Newspapering at

The Bluffton News-Banner

Many of the changes that occurred during the 1950's were fueled by World War II. The war was concluded in 1945 and American soldiers began returning home, eight million of them. Most wanted to get their life back and that usually meant getting a house, a family and a car. The demand for housing and cars stimulated American manufacturing and propelled a business boom the likes of which had never been seen before. British historian Robert Payne visited America in 1949 and afterwards wrote about America, "She sits bestrides the world like a Colossus; no other power at any time in the world's history has possessed so varied or so great an influence on other nations . . . Half of the wealth of the world, more than half of the productivity, nearly two thirds of the world's machines are concentrated in American hands; the rest of the world lies in the shadow of American industry."

American car companies quickly returned from manufacturing war material and began to turn out cars for the war-starved public. The first post- war car designs were based on engineering work that was completed before the outbreak of war. Consequently, the late 40's designs looked like cars that had been built before the war. By 1950 Harvey Earl of General Motors had designed a new Cadillac with fins and tail lights that were reminiscent of the P38 aircraft and the look caught on. The result was that General Motors couldn't build cars fast enough to satisfy demand. This design feature reached a peak with the introduction of the 1957 Chevrolet with its pronounced fins and General Motors built over 50% of all cars sold in America.

GM had a pronounced affect on politics as well as industry. One of the engineering leaders of General Motors, Charlie Wilson, left GM to work for President Eisenhower as Secretary of Defense. Wilson was widely quoted as saying that "what was good for GM was good for the country". Many people thought that way as General Motors surged forward with new car designs that captured people's hearts and ultimately led to domination of the American car industry as both Ford and Chrysler gave way to the highest volume producer in the world.

Another legacy of the war was improvements to the American highway system. In the 1930's Adolph Hitler needed a massive public works project to put Germans to work following the economic depression that had gripped Europe and especially Germany. Hitler decided to build a new kind of highway, the Autobahn, which was unsurpassed anywhere in the world. The highway was remarkable for its time with its banked curves, limited access, and separation of lanes in opposite directions by a generous grass-covered median that allowed safe travel at high speeds. One of the admirers of the German Autobahn and critic of American highways was Dwight Eisenhower. Eisenhower had conducted a convoy across America when he was a young officer and so he knew the terrible condition of many American roads and he determined to do something about it when he became President.

American roads were built over many years primarily to facilitate trade. Many of the roads followed prior Indian paths and they meandered around hills, streams and any other obstacle that a man on foot or horseback could avoid by making a turn here or there. The result was a mishmash of roads that went in bewildering directions from one city to the next. The roads were improved only nominally as farmers sought means to take their produce to market and as asphalt and concrete became generally available at reasonable cost. This was the situation when President Eisenhower championed the National Highway Act in 1956 and the new Interstate Highway System began to make automotive travel in America much, much easier.

The effect of Eisenhower's road programs had a far-reaching impact across the nation. Two new businesses that began in the 50's owe their success directly to the American fascination with vehicle travel: MacDonald's and their hamburgers and Holiday Inns with their low cost, high quality standardized rooms for rent. Both these enterprises began small, developed into mega-businesses and spawned an entire industry of like businesses that continue to succeed today.

The combined effect of affordable automobiles, high wages and improved highways forever altered the landscape of America in ways that no one could have imagined. The availability of cars and trucks that were affordable for the middle class prompted a change like Pandora's Box. Slowly, the importance of towns and villages were diminished as transportation improved. The ubiquitous railroads began to suffer as travel by train or interurban (an interurban was a self propelled train car that traveled between cities) was less important since nearly every family had access to a car. Living in or near a city became less important since one could easily commute. Businesses no longer worried about a having a convenient location in town since an automobile could easily bring customers to the store regardless of where it was located. And, why not build your house next to a pretty stream or on a wooded lot and never mind that it happened to be miles from work or school when the family car could carry the new homeowners wherever they wanted to go.

Since everyone had begun traveling by car, stores now needed large parking lots that were not available in town. The rural areas suddenly offered a special benefit to the new generation who no longer wanted to walk from store to store since they were becoming accustomed to mostly 'butt time' during travel. Stores began moving out of town and new subdivisions sprang from fields that had been used for tomatoes and corn for generations. Suburban sprawl took root and blossomed before most knew what had happened.

During the 1950's Bluffton had a glimpse of things to come with the start of suburban sprawl. The place was just outside the city limits on the north side of the Wabash River along the main north-south road, State Road 1. It was known as Villa North and it was an area of businesses and former farmhouses fronting corn fields that stretched along the highway for a mile or more. The city fathers enabled the growth to the north (as they always do) by providing city services to those who requested them, despite the cost of longer sewer lines, etc. Neither the houses nor the businesses were close together and so it was a lousy place for a paper route. The News-Banner, like the city fathers, couldn't resist the pull of additional commerce, so they decided to make a paper route in Villa North, reducing their profit by providing a higher than normal profit for the paper boy who had to travel further for fewer customers. That was the route my brother Jim had for several years while I plodded around town on my city paper route.

Jim graduated from High School in 1958 and announced his plan to join the Navy. The News-Banner wondered if I wanted to take over the coveted Villa North route since it had been in my family for some years while Jim had the route. I decided no, but under pressure from my family, I finally acquiesced to take over the higher paying route. The problem, as I saw it, was that I would be required to ride my bike along State Road 1 in clear view of my friends. I, a respected member of the Hi-Y, a high school student nearing adulthood, would be forced to ride my lousy bike up and down the lousy road delivering papers like a young kid in short pants. The only saving grace about the whole thing was the better money and my Grandpa.

Grandpa Tudor was a Bluffton area house painter. He had made a respectable living for a number of years painting houses in town but now age was catching up to him and his painting jobs were fewer and fewer. One of the ways he passed his time was helping on the Villa North paper route. At first, he would show up at the newspaper office whenever it was raining and he would hoist my bike in the back of his pick-up truck and off we would go to Villa North, me in passenger seat with the window down to load the mailboxes with my papers. Then, as time went on he began showing up more frequently to help with the route. He seemed to enjoy it and I never objected to passing my papers from the front seat of his truck instead of my lousy bike. The hardest part of the Villa North route was seeing my high school

111

classmates passing by in their cars. I always tried to be looking away when they passed but sometimes seeing them and waving while I was on my bike was unavoidable; during those times my face burned with shame at my lowly place in the cosmos.

The idea of going to college slowly took root in my mind and the Villa North paper route was an excellent opportunity to bank funds for college. Since no one in my family had ever attended college, the idea of college and its cost was something of a mystery. I only knew one person that I could talk with who had gone to college and he had borrowed funds to support his college training at a Christian-based school, so he wasn't helpful in explaining about the cost. My mother and dad both encouraged saving as a general principal and so I used the largest share of my paper route profits for my college fund. It turned out to be a wise idea in the years to come.

I continued on the Villa North route after my brother went off to the Navy for my first years in high school and then a funny thing happened: The News Banner offered me an after-school job inside the print shop for the paper. I thought it was a dream job, decomposing the lead type that made the news print for the day's paper, carrying the lead to the melt pot and supplying lead bars to the linotype machines and helping with the newspaper distribution by carrying papers to the post office. I earned $ 1.35 per hour, more than I thought possible. Of course I said yes to the new job and started working each day after school and most of Saturday. It was fun and I felt like a real newsman. (A curious thing was that Jim had studied printing in school, a key part of which was the use of linotype machines. Linotype machines were like giant typewriters except the output was a line of type embossed on a thin lead strip that was exactly the width of one column of newsprint. The high school taught this vocational work to one class of students each year – 25 to 30 students- yet there were only 5 linotype jobs in the entire town.)

I learned a lot about the newspaper business but even more important, I learned a lot about people. I worked at the News Banner for the rest of my high school career and for the first part of my college years under the supervision of several people; actually, everyone seemed to be my boss and my job included a wide variety of tasks that could change at a moment's notice. One of the most important lessons I learned was the necessity of satisfying whoever was the boss at the moment.

The big boss of the newspaper was the majority owner, publisher and editor, Roger Swaim. I thought Swaim was the most important person in Bluffton, based the way that both ordinary people and the important people in town treated him. The principal of the high school, for example, worked part time for the newspaper in managing the accounting work, a fact that impressed me as the boss of all the teachers at school was subservient to the boss at the newspaper.

Roger Swaim was a big, barrel-shaped man and he liked to eat. He prowled around town in the evenings looking for news stories with his notepad at the ready. His beat was the restaurants. He went from one place to another and ordered a malted or a sundae while looking for news tips. Often his last restaurant stop was an order for a Pepto-Bismol.

Swaim had interesting personal habits that those of us who worked for him had to know about. He was fastidious about cleanliness and he sometimes walked through the print shop with his ever-present white handkerchief in hand, dusting the shelves as he walked by. Since it was my job to help clean up the place each evening after the decomposing job, I always figured he was sending me a message when he walked with his handkerchief out. In response to his handkerchief display, for the next several days I would dust the shelves that he walked by.

Roger smoked cigars and he was rarely without one in hand. His office was thick with cigar smoke and you could tell when he was coming by the smell of his cigar. Since he nearly always had a cigar burning, he generated a lot of cigar butts. Roger was particular about his appearance; he always wore a suit with a matching necktie and a freshly pressed white shirt and he gave the impression that his personal hygiene was beyond criticism. However; like many other smokers he seemed to think that the outdoors was a trash area for his cigar butts and so he routinely tossed his out the front door of his office. Once, the businessmen on either side of the newspaper office began kidding him about his practice to let him know they were getting tired of stepping over his trash. I was promptly dispatched to sweep the sidewalk and the gutter for his used butts. He quit tossing them out after that.

The newspaper business was a one block building in the downtown business district with its front office and front door on Market Street. The rear door was the entry to the print shop at the back of the long brown building. The building was bordered on either side by bustling businesses: an old-fashioned grocery run by two brothers on one side and a thriving Montgomery-Ward (Monkey Ward to some) on the other. Since the newspaper office was centrally located, there were always pedestrians about and Roger managed to keep the newspaper business visible to all those potential customers.

The front office had large windows and Roger used them to advantage. Just behind the windows in full view of passersby stood the UPI teletype that busily banged out the national and international news stories of the day. Of course, you couldn't read the print from outside but you had the impression that the newspaper was on guard for the latest news. If some local news of importance occurred, Roger would tape a large sheet of paper to the window noting the event and the likely headline in that day's paper. "In the public interest," Roger would say.

Bluffton Court House, built in 1889

During elections and after important basketball games, I was pressed into service for the paper as a carrier of news. I would be positioned at the court house to receive the election counts and then dispatched to the newspaper office to carry the news and post the big sheet of paper on the office window. After basketball games, Roger would pay me to answer the telephone to give out the late night basketball scores to callers. "In the public interest," Roger would say. It took me quite a while to understand that it was also in the interest of the newspaper.

The newspaper was an essential part of town and involved one way or another, in all the activities that took place in and around the community. Working there made me feel connected to the town. Since there were only a dozen employees in the shop and another half dozen in the office, working for the paper provoked a feeling of teamwork and camaraderie with the other employees. It was a great experience and one that helped me on a fast start for the rest of my life's journey.

117

Chapter 13

Upperclassman

The decade of the 1950's saw expanding technology that forever changed America. Television, the Salk polio vaccine, new transportation and improved household appliances all leapt forward with a speed that dumbfounded the older generation. It seemed to me that our life in Bluffton was like riding a teeter-totter oscillating between new technology and the old ways. The older folks all seemed to embrace the old ways while my classmates and I were eager for the best of the newest.

One of the older practices that started giving way in the fifties was the amount and type of personal service that was commonly available. Some richer folks hired maids and others hired ladies like my grandmother to work on a part-time basis as a housekeeper. Other examples of personal services that are now largely gone were attendants at gas stations who washed car windows while pumping gas, and the milkman who delivered fresh milk to our door each day.

The old style grocery stores were another victim of the changes wrought in the fifties. It was still possible in the late 1950's to send your order to the grocery and the clerk would pick the groceries, wrap them and deliver them to your home. This service came at a price; however, and the new supermarket in Villa North offered lower priced groceries provided you selected what you wanted and carried them to your vehicle without asking their help. Many folks favored the lower prices and wide selections available at the supermarket and the heyday of the small grocery came to an end.

Many of my family friends and relatives seemed stuck in the old world while those of us in my generation couldn't get enough of television, electric coffee-makers and hot-rod cars. My next door neighbor Ida Moser was forever mired in the old times as she longed for a return of the iceman to fill the icebox that sat idle on her porch. Some of my rural family relatives still used their old privy, and television was still a novelty to my grandparents who seemed to care little for the contraption. "What is it good for?" my Grandpa Ora asked whenever the subject was raised.

As the decade of the fifties came to a close I became an upperclassman. I was working at the newspaper every day after school and the sometimes late night work made it important for me to have my own transportation. My parents consented to my buying a car of my own. When I first went to high school it was every other boy's dream to have his own car. By the time I actually needed a car, it didn't seem as important to me beyond the practical necessity – something, I don't know what, had changed. I was now more focused on work and college, although my girlfriend was a close second and the car afforded us some much needed privacy.

My best buddy at this time was Gene Rice. Gene was a taller, polite, dark haired young man, who was an avid euchre player and frequent visitor to the card table, otherwise known as our kitchen table. Gene and I spent a lot of time together both before and after Brother Jim left for the Navy and we had many adventures including a few that yielded lasting reminders.

Gene was a hard working guy who managed to buy a late model Oldsmobile convertible. He was usually the driver on summer nights and we had great times with the top down on his car. One of the foolish things we did was speed down the highway while one or more of the passengers would stand erect to feel the full blast of the rushing air. We couldn't let it end there. No siree, not us.

On one occasion I remember SITTING on the door frame with one leg dangling outside the car and the other resting inside. For some unknown reason, the driver spiked the brake. I recall doing a forward flip in the air before I landed on the ground with a noteworthy drip of blood coming from a spot under my chin. I still have the scar.

Gene and I also had a noteworthy adventure during the summer after Brother Jim joined the Navy. Somehow, we talked our parents into the idea of the two of us driving cross country to Norfolk, Virginia to visit Jim over the course of a week. I was 16 and Gene was either 17 or 18 years old. We drove in Gene's convertible and stayed in a YMCA in Norfolk while visiting Jim. It was a memorable trip; hotter than blazes and impressive to visit the Navy base in Norfolk that some called the hell-hole of America. Norfolk catered to the sailors. Their main street featured tattoo parlors, strip joints and bars. The sailors on board ships stationed at Norfolk didn't have far to travel to find ways to spend their money and lose their naïveté.

Jim's ship, a repair vessel, spent most of it's time in dock in Norfolk so he got to know Norfolk pretty well. He showed us the local sights and took us to the beach. We also visited one of his buddies who had a wife and a house in Norfolk and I learned that the cultural norm among sailors seemed to be that offering a shot of whiskey to a 16 year old was accepted behavior. I did my best not to spill my cookies. Nothing untoward happened during the visit and Gene and I made it home safely and a little bit wiser.

When I became an upperclassman I began spending time with one of the girls that was in some of my classes. The girl was Norma Rice, Gene's younger sister. She and I became attracted as we shared some classes and the result was that we began to spend time together. Pretty soon we were trading notes in the hallway and sitting together in Study Hall. I invited her to the Junior/Senior High School Prom which was about the most important social event of the year. The Prom included a dinner that was served in the high school gymnasium followed by the highlight, a dance with live entertainment.

Pretty soon we were going steady. We went to the movies, an occasional party (where she danced and I watched) and we did the other things that moonstruck teenagers do. I managed to keep my friendship with Norma and Gene in separate compartments. It worked. It was almost like the two of them lived separately so far as our mutual relationship was concerned. Norma and I had the normal high school relationship until she and I each

Norma Rice

121

separated at the end of high school for different colleges. She told me we had to break up before college as her mother insisted. I don't know why her mother insisted on us parting, I supposed her mother was hoping she would find someone of more promise than me.

We never spoke again after our parting at the end of high school. After college she married and moved to the southwest where she gained some relief from the asthma that plagued her much of her life. Sadly, she fell victim to cancer and complications from her treatment ended her life prematurely.

The end of high school came quickly, almost before I was ready. I had gradually adopted the idea of college as most of my classmates in the academic curricula had done, but I had little idea of what I should study. I decided to wait until college began to make that decision. The tearful separation from Norma, high school graduation and plans for college seemed to come in rapid-fire bursts interspersed between my continuing work at the News-Banner.

I decided to attend college in Fort Wayne, Indiana where I could continue to live at home and avoid dormitory costs for a year or two. High School graduation was in spring 1961 and I started college in the fall of that year. College occupied all my time for the first several semesters. I found the studies absorbing and I soon made the decision to study Chemistry instead of the course work in Forestry that I began. I spent three years at the Purdue University extension in Fort Wayne before it was necessary to transfer to the main campus of Purdue University in Lafayette, Indiana.

In the fall of 1964, I packed up my 1956 light blue Chevrolet and set out on my journey to Purdue for my final course work for my B.S. Degree. I had clothes, a little money, a plan, and a cultural underpinning from family, friends, teachers, relatives and countless others who represented Bluffton and Wells County in the period of the late 1940's through the 1950's. I left Bluffton and Wells County that sunny afternoon, not imagining that I would never return to live there again.

The old African proverb that 'it takes a village to raise a child' is indeed true. I didn't realize it at the time, but I when I left home that last time, I was equipped with a compass learned at the hands of Roger Swaim, The Wesleyan Church, family and classmates, and in fact, the entire experience of my childhood in Bluffton. Unknown to me at the time, the things I learned then formed the basis for my I work and behavior throughout my life. Truly, I became what I was then.

So, Bluffton was my hometown. The place I grew up, the place I sometimes think about and dream about, the place where I was told was the best place in the whole word to grow up. It is the kind of place that sticks with you even 50 years later. I understand now, about my cousin Mike Flowers who grew up in Bluffton, but like me, lived the rest of his life elsewhere. When his death became imminent and he understood, he made his wishes known: He wanted to be buried in his hometown of Bluffton.

THE END

Made in United States
North Haven, CT
14 December 2023

45541510R00068